THE ENTREPRENEUR'S BLUEPRINT TO MASSIVE SUCCESS

*Creating An Exceptional Lifestyle While Doing Business On **YOUR** Terms*

Peter Voogd

ISBN PAPERBACK: 978-0-9909973-2-0

ISBN HARDCOVER: 978-0-9909973-3-7

Cover design: Hugo Fernandez, Just Digital INC.

Interior design: Hugo Fernandez, Just Digital INC.

Editing: Kelly Stokes Brown, KSB Marketing Message.

Printed in the USA

Praise for "The Entrepreneurs Blueprint"

"The best content to help you get to the next level"

"This content is for not only young entrepreneurs, but for anybody looking to take their life and business to the next level. Having worked closely with Peter Voogd for nearly half a decade, and seeing his evolution as a highly successful Entrepreneur is very inspiring. I had high expectations for this book. All were exceeded."

~ Hal Elrod — Best Selling Author of the Miracle Morning

"One of the best"

"I used to think I had to get an MBA or spend a lot of money on a coach in order to get practical business advice and strategies. But the advice Peter gives it some of the most valuable I've heard in a long time. I've managed to increase my Business and productivity just by taking Peters advice."

~ James Carney

"A life saver!"

"I am totally addicted to this content! It's by far some of the best content out - full of actionable items. I love that Peter is clear, concise and gives no BS. This information is absolutely mind blowing and life-changing, and it's the number one book I recommend to everyone looking to up their business big-time. Thank you so much, Peter Voogd, for offering your insight, experience and strategies. I am extremely grateful that you are in my life."

~ Susan Adams

"A breath of fresh perspective"

"Peter tells it how it is. This book will change your perspective and really bring clarity to your life. I wanted to find out how to be successful and this is exactly what Peter teaches in each chapter. I am forever changed because of Peter and thankful for his devotion to providing very, very valuable information."

~ Bradley Duncan

"If you only read one book, make it this"

"I can't imagine driving around without making Peter pushing me to grow every day. There's so much content out there today, we get overwhelmed and are put in information consumption paralysis, learning and learning without ever taking the time to implement anything, afraid of missing out on the next best. Peter brings the very best from the top minds in growth and development, and shares the key points in actionable ways. I have absorbed a massive amount of content, but nothing pushed me to see more growth and results than Peter's content. Thank you, truly."

~ Kevin Gilpin

"Game Changing"

"I'm just amazed how much value I get from listening to Peter. This content is perfect for anyone who's tired of living a mediocre life, and for people who want to get serious about what they want and need for their lives. Ultimately, it is your choice to change, but leave it up to Peter to reassure you that it is the right choice!"

~ Cassie Cholaki

"Best advice for aspiring entrepreneurs"

"If you're an aspiring entrepreneur and you're looking to take your businesses to a place you've haven't imagined before, this is definitely the book you need to read. ASAP. Even if you don't consider yourself an entrepreneur but you just want to get more out of life and be successful and fulfilled, this podcast has got the goods. Peter is literally giving away the key is to wealth, success and happiness. Most of the lessons are short, so I like the fact that it does not take up a huge chunk of my time, and they are still filled with intensely practical and actionable steps to take. because I have six classes in school and am involved in other school activities, I only have a few hours a week to work; but by using tips in this podcast I've gone from making a few hundred a month to a couple thousand a month – and now I have a clear picture of how to make millions when I graduate and focus on the effort on my business. Every week I implement something in this book and it has made a huge difference in my own personal goals and success with school, my business, in my life."

~ Alexander James Campbell

Contents

ABOUT THE AUTHOR: PETER VOOGD

A Visionary, Game Changer, Speaker, Author, Mentor, and Dedicated Entrepreneur, Peter Voogd is on a mission to shift our culture, and won't stop until his vision becomes a reality. He's seen a lot of success at an early age, but he's seen even more failure. He's used his past to design his ideal future, and has dedicated the last 11 years to helping Entrepreneurs exponentially grow their income while deepening their network so they can live life on THEIR terms. He's been labeled the thought leader for millennials because he *is* one, he has succeeded as one, and has been successful leading an organization comprising of millennials to the highest level. He has an authentic and raw understanding of what it takes to motivate and inspire the leaders of today, because of his real experience and background. He has trained and led close to 5,000 Sales Reps, Managers, College Students, Professionals, Business Owners, Olympians and many others to high levels of success.

He went from a negative bank balance to over 100,000 in the bank at age 23, and learned how to double that while scaling back hours worked. He then took the same formula and applied it in another industry. He strongly believes that, the more people you help to succeed, the more successful you become, and is a firm believer that 95% of society takes what is given rather than designing and creating the ideal future.

Peter has started a movement to empower America's Aspiring Entrepreneurs and Young Professionals called ***The Game Changers Academy***. It has quickly become one of the most Prestigious Training and Networking Communities in the world, and continues to attract

Professionals and Ambitious Entrepreneurs from all over the Country. He understands on a deep level that the Entrepreneur is the future of our society.

He is also the Founder of one of iTunes top podcasts "***The Young Entrepreneur Lifestyle Podcast,***" which is focused on bringing results, guidance, and excellence to entrepreneurs worldwide. It's helping entrepreneurs do business and live life on their terms.

Enjoy the journey and keep us posted with all your success. Peter loves connecting with like-minded people, so connect with him!

Facebook: PeterVoogd23

LinkedIn: Peter Voogd

Twitter: PeterVoogd23

Instagram: Ambition23

Google+: Peter Voogd

FREE BOOK GUIDE

As a thank you for purchasing *"The Entrepreneur Blueprint to Massive Success"* and taking action to start living life on YOUR terms, Peter has assembled a series of valuable tools you can use to help you maximize your entrepreneurial experience and overall productivity.

Sure, he could have offered you some BS special report like most 'online marketers,' but he'd rather give you something practical that will help you move your business forward and help you become the most productive person you know ASAP.

He's created a deep dive action guide to help you master the content on the following pages. You can download this special action guide for free at:

www.TheEntrepreneurBreakthrough.com/Guide

I

Introduction

"None are more hopelessly enslaved than those who falsely believe they are free."

~ Johann Wolfgang Von Goethe

The Entrepreneur's Blueprint was created to help you thrive by giving you the tools and strategies needed to elevate every area of your life and business. What does it really mean to live life on YOUR terms? It means doing things when you want, wherever you want, and with whomever you want. It's having the power of choices. There is only one real success, and that's to be able to live life on your terms, your own way. In a world filled with BS, sometimes the things you don't want to hear are the things you need to hear the most. That's why "**The Young Entrepreneur Lifestyle**" movement was created, and continues to impact millions around the world. In the pages following we share the 30 most powerful lessons you must learn to become the best at what you do, and thrive at the highest level. You'll find action steps, thought provoking questions, and team activities to help you spark your mind and maximize your productivity as an entrepreneur, sales professional, and leader.

One of the goals of this book is to get you to think, and not just think, but to expand your awareness as an entrepreneur. The story of the human race is the story of men and women selling themselves short, settling for far less than they are truly capable of. The truth is we're all meant to thrive and be 100% free. We came into this world with more talents and abilities than most of us ever use, but our potential is only drawn from us when we are focused on our strengths, and embrace who we really are. As you increase your intelligence you start to realize how much turmoil our society is really in, and the lack of freedom most people are oblivious to.

There is nothing worse than living a life somebody else designed for you. The system is designed so the majority fail, which is exactly what they are doing. My hope is that this book reaches those in need of a reality check or some "realness" in a world filled with BS and sugarcoating. Here are some of the tragedies of living life below your real potential, and settling.

Guaranteed Regret

"The two most important days in a person's life are the day they were born, and the day they find out why."

~John Maxwell

The number one regret from people on their deathbeds is that they settled for what others expected of them because they were never brave enough to pursue their dreams. When they look back at their lives, what stood out the most was their unattained goals and aspirations. They are often haunted by decisions that resulted in the lives they ended up with. The likelihood of regret is drastically increased when you're trying to fit into others' expectations of you. The more you settle, the more regret you will eventually have.

Minimal Experiences

Ultimately life is an adventure. Experiences and memories are what separate the elite lives from the mediocre. After studying countless world-class people it's clear they are constantly creating memorable experiences. What's the point of doing something if you're not having fun, and it doesn't elevate your emotional frequency? Why not take a mini-adventure (half-day/weekend) every 5-7 days? This shakes you out of any complacency, which is the WORST thing on earth. Build out your adventures at the beginning of the year, and make sure you always have trips planned for your future. According to cnn.com, 76% of our society is currently living paycheck to paycheck. It's tough to create exceptional experiences with minimal pay. Money does matter, as we will see throughout this book.

Toxic Relationships

Mediocrity loves mediocrity, and misery really does love company. There are way too many haters, bullshitters, and quitters hating on the go-getters, and those striving for greatness. When you stay away from mediocrity and toxic people it makes an immediate difference in your personal energy, peace of mind, and motivation level. Yet so many people hang on to those who complain, bitch, moan, play victim ("why does this always happen to me?", they say), and continue settling for less than they are capable of. It's your job to make sure your past is brighter than your future, and the people you surround yourself with believe in you, encourage you, and raise your standards. Grant Cardone reminded me a couple weeks ago that "if you still have all the same friends you had in high school you probably haven't grown very much." Ouch. If you're moving closer to your dreams, while most are moving towards mediocrity you're bound to run into haters. I'd strongly recommend dropping all communication with those who don't make you feel exceptional this year. Life is way too short.

A Mediocre Legacy

"The wealthiest place on the planet is the cemetery, because it's filled with brilliant ideas, potential... all wasted."

~ Tony Robbins

The worst thing in the world: leaving a trail of mediocrity behind you. You rarely see a legendary entrepreneur who had mediocre parents, unless they found a great mentor along the way. At some point you must realize it's not about just you, it's about those you inspire, those who look up to you, and those counting on you. 71% of people hate what they do and are actively *disengaged* at work. If you don't like what you do even 1% it's time to STEP UP and make some changes. The more you settle, the more you regret. You only get this life ONCE, don't spend it doing things you hate. With every text, every word, every tweet, and every action you are creating your legacy.

Most people just talk about success, wish they had success, but never take the necessary action consistently to achieve it. They spend year after year just trying to get by versus designing a compelling future. When you follow the steps outlined in this book, complete the activities, and focus on mastering the content, you'll forever change your mindset about how you live your life and what you're truly capable of achieving. You'll move from merely surviving to thriving in this new economy. Pay it forward and share this book with the world, because the greatest satisfaction in life comes from helping others fulfill their potential.

II

Life and Business on <u>YOUR</u> Terms

I am a serial entrepreneur. It all began when I was 14 years old with an eBay business. I was fascinated by this new online world and how easy it was to make money by selling goods online. eBay introduced me to a whole new way of looking at work, making a living and fulfilling my lifestyle expectations.

My dad owned a construction company and a lot of my friends worked for him. I never liked the idea of hard labor. When my dad asked me to work for him, I would do everything I could to get out of it. I worked for about a half hour for him one day and that was enough for me to realize that I was not going to make a living in construction. One of my friends worked for him. He would work eight-hour days and only make about $60 per day. He shoveled and hauled sand up a hill all day and was content with his minimum wage job. I knew I could never be content with the income or the hard labor of a regular job. I remember checking my eBay account a few days after I helped my dad, and I had made $91 without any hard labor. That was my first "a-ha" moment, and it showed me the potential of being an entrepreneur.

However, even though I saw another way to make money, I was conditioned by everybody around me to get a "real" job. I grew up in a small retirement community of eight thousand people. The adults, students, and my friends all had normal jobs. So, at 18, I took the same road because I thought that was the way everyone had to start.

My first job was valeting cars at a local casino. I may have lacked the love of hard labor, but I worked hard as a valet and provided a high level of customer service. However, at the end of the month, I would add up my paychecks and feel disappointed. I'd work 40 hours a week and barely make enough money to cover my bills.

I would look at each paycheck and ask myself what I could do to increase my income based on my value and my work ethic. I soon realized that I wasn't getting paid based on my value as a person or my work ethic; I was getting paid based on someone else's idea of my value. Not only that, but my schedule was completely controlled by someone else. This just didn't make sense to me. I had no control over my income, my future potential income, or my schedule. I felt unemployable. Can you relate?

That's when I realized I wanted something different than what I saw around me. I wanted complete control over my hours and my pay. So, I quit. And that was the end of having a "real" job for me. I knew what I was looking for and sought out an opportunity in direct sales because I saw quickly that I would be paid based on my potential and on what I created versus what someone thought I was worth. I worked hard and I was really passionate about creating my own destiny and my own income. I was successful and people were noticing my results, so much so that people were reaching out to me and my company and asking what I was doing to get those results. I slowly transitioned into teaching and the leadership side of sales. I wanted to build my own sales team instead of doing the selling myself. I was soon offered an opportunity to become a manager and run my own organization. I was only 21, a senior in college, when I opened my first office.

Later that same year, I was presented with another opportunity to open my own district with the same direct sales company. The only caveat was I had to move from Eugene, Oregon to the Seattle area. All of my friends were graduating. It was May and everyone was pumped up about going to the beach or the pool and having fun. And here I was, getting ready to move to a new city and run a district office, on my own.

You can imagine how I felt. I started having second thoughts and doubts about taking this opportunity. I thought maybe I shouldn't be doing this; that I should be with my friends and having fun. But then I reminded myself what I really wanted was a different lifestyle and I wanted a challenge. So I left my circle of friends and moved to Seattle to start my business. That was the toughest decision I've ever made.

Here's the thing about taking risks. I failed miserably. I had no business experience. While I had studied business in college, I had no practical experience in running a business. I constantly used the excuses, "Oh, this isn't for me," "This is the wrong area," "I didn't get trained well," and "It's not my fault." The reality was, I was working 80 hours a week, stressed out, broke, and living in a one-bedroom apartment with the only furniture being a mattress. It was the lowest point in my life. I remember trying to scrounge money just to buy food. All of those doubts came flooding back. Everyone told me starting a business was too risky, and not to do it. But I had also learned something very valuable: The toughest decisions, the ones that hurt in the moment, are the best ones for your future, for your lifestyle, and for your vision.

Taking risks and experiencing low points will challenge you. However, they also offer a window of opportunity, of change, that you may not otherwise encounter. During my low point, I turned that frustration and discouragement into motivation. I started reading through notes that I took at one of the seminars I attended. I came across a quote that really stuck with me: "If you want to be a millionaire, talk to billionaires, because you'll get there quicker." Then I started to think about the people I was surrounding myself with…

I dedicated myself to studying, learning, and reading about personal development, entrepreneurship and successful CEOs. I also hired a mentor. The investment in the mentor was steep, so I had to borrow some money at first. Ironically, the decision to hire a mentor and borrow the money to pay for this investment cemented in me a strong desire to never struggle with money again.

The year I hired my mentor was the same year I went from broke to a six figure income. I was doing well financially but guess what I didn't have? My freedom. I was still working 80 hours per week and I started to question if this was really what entrepreneurship was all about.

What if you had the time, flexibility, and lifestyle you desired, but no energy?

I had money, but no time to spend it or enjoy time with my family. This prompted me to read and study even more. I wanted to learn from entrepreneurs who had attained a lifestyle of working minimally, made a lot of money and were able to spend time doing what they wanted. I read 50 of the best books on the most successful CEOs and entrepreneurs. I started reaching out to the top people in my company and asking them how they were able to reach their business and lifestyle goals. I dedicated that entire year to figuring out how these big CEOs and the top entrepreneurs were making millions, yet also had free time.

The following year, I was able to double my sales, and scale back from working 80 hours to about 20 hours all due to what I had learned during the past year. I was beginning to build the life I really wanted. While building a sales team, I continued to reach out to high-level people. My ultimate goal was to make every year bigger than my last.

After a few years of growth, great income, new connections, and knowledge from running my own sales team, I felt the magnitude of my mission growing. The people I wanted to inspire and work with were the young entrepreneurs, those 5 to 10% of people who are hungry for a better life and who don't want to take the traditional route. I'm talking about those dedicated enough to invest in themselves and take action, not the 90% who talk a great game, but don't back it up.

I was already leading and inspiring people on my team and I knew there was a way to reach more people and help them reach their personal and professional goals. My next question was: What can I create, and what can I dedicate my life to that will make a big difference, not only locally, but also in the world? I knew I needed to expand; however, I also knew this would mean taking another big risk. Are you starting to see a pattern?

I decided to leave what I was doing and create something on a much bigger scale. I noticed people were struggling with the amount of information and it was paralyzing entrepreneurs. I wanted to be the person who guided entrepreneurs to the results, to the lifestyle, and to the legacy they wanted to create. I left a very consistent business working 15 to 20 hours a week, and earning a very nice six figures because I knew there was something more for me. Settling is the death of all real ambition.

That decision, that risk, led me to create **realVIPsuccess.com**, which includes free resources to bring excellence to entrepreneurs worldwide, to start the **Game Changers Academy**, and of course, **The Young Entrepreneur Lifestyle** podcast. I dedicate myself purely to helping entrepreneurs reach their highest potential and also help them bring out their creative genius. Over the years, I've learned how to make massive changes in income, lifestyle and business revenue. I not only have tactical things to share, but experience, stories, and perspectives that bring about a higher level of life satisfaction and real tangible results – both personally and professionally. If you are serious about success and entrepreneurship, I can show you how to achieve your biggest goals and ultimately, your lifestyle dreams.

I'll share my secret revelations I've had through my struggles and through my successes to build wealth and a great lifestyle. The one thing I know for sure is you need new information, new knowledge, and new ideas you haven't heard before to take your business and your life to the next level. When I started focusing on education and bettering myself, I experienced success very quickly. I realized too, the only limitations I had were in my own mind, and when my habits started to match my goals, everything became possible. If you are willing to dedicate yourself to learning and to following this blueprint, you'll see that you have all the power and the ability to achieve anything you wish.

My focus is on mastery versus information overload. I've done hundreds of hours of research, spent thousands of dollars on high level mastermind seminars, mentorships, programs, coaches, and I've failed and failed again. But ultimately, I've experienced great success. I know what it takes to succeed and I know the pitfalls to avoid. I've taken all the information I've learned and simplified it into actionable steps and provided tactical advice you can use in your business and in your life to lead to amazing results. A smart person learns from their mistakes, as all successful people do; but those who want real success learn from other people's mistakes to shorten the learning curve—by not making the same mistakes and wasting as much time or money.

You'll learn the tactical tips, the experience, and the mindset it takes to build the ideal lifestyle based on who you are, what your core values are, and what you want versus taking what's given or expected. If you are ready to differentiate yourself from the rest of society and live a life few ever attain, you're ready for this book.

This book isn't about storing a lot of information. This book is about taking guided action to improve your life and business. When reading this book, make sure you're in a place where you can focus and implement the information into your life and business quickly so you can start seeing real results.

Chapter II Action Steps

1. Know what you want. If you are still wavering in your mind about what you want, don't go to the next chapter. Stop and get clear about what you want first. Write it down and be very specific about what you want and WHY.

2. Be willing to dedicate yourself to learning and growing. Use the information and the action steps in this book. Commit to implementing what you learn, even if you only use one action step at first. Practice, practice, practice.

3. Be willing to take risks. As an entrepreneur, or even as a business professional, you must get comfortable with risk. To really stand out and succeed in any endeavor, you have to be willing to break the mold and do things differently. Commit to doing one thing differently this week.

III

The Highest Form of Accomplishment

There is a wave of overwhelm and overload sweeping over our society. There's an infinite amount of information available to us at all times. In fact, the influx of information from the past five years is more than the previous 40 years combined! Not only are people getting overwhelmed, they're also stuck in inaction. This is where having a focused mindset makes all the difference.

In achieving goals and dreams, mindset comes first and results come second. If you really want big results, you have to start with your mindset. If you are constantly taking on new information, but you are not clear and guided in how this information will move your life or your business forward, you are going to fail. You must be clear, focused and choose guided learning that moves you closer to your goals. This really helped me early in my career and was part of my first breakthrough in business. I call it, The Mastery Versus Overload Principle.

Mastery is the highest form of accomplishment. The only way to really become successful is to master the fundamentals that are matched with your end results and goals. Most people have so much information – they read the books, they go to conferences or seminars, they have three coaches, they search online, they watch YouTube videos, they buy programs, and they're completely overwhelmed because they don't know how to apply any of the information to their lives or their businesses. We can all relate to this feeling of overload, right? Even with something as simple as the massive amount of emails you dread having to sift through or even take the time to read can be overwhelming. Therefore, it's imperative that you develop a mastery mindset! This way you can stay focused on your goals, and on what you'll commit to learn, so you can improve your business. You have to clear out all distractions. The key to avoiding overload is learning to block distractions and focus only on clear, guided learning and select information that is beneficial to you and your goals.

The way I see it, there are only two kinds of learners. The first kind of learner wants to get as much information as possible as fast as they can. They rarely implement what they learn and they often remain unchanged financially and personally over time. This isn't because they don't want to change; it's because they haven't developed a mastery mindset. The second kind of learner is deliberate with both what they study, but more importantly, with what they apply. They focus on a new skill or new idea until they've adopted it and have improved results before they go to the next skill or idea.

One of our members in the Game Changers Academy was doing extremely well, but a couple months ago, he came to me and said, "Peter, my manager and a lot of people around me are going to read 50 books this year. I'm super excited! What do you think about that?" I told him my honest opinion: it wasn't a good idea. I suggested he focus on picking 3 books that are the most congruent with his end result and master those 3, versus reading 50 that he could never be able to apply. He's been doing as I suggested over the last couple of months, and he said this one tip has been a game changer for him. I knew another guy who claimed to have read 50 books. I reached out to him to see what he learned. When I asked him what his biggest takeaways were or what he gained after reading so many books, he couldn't remember anything about the books at all. He did say, "My motivation went up, and I did a little bit better than the year before." Imagine if he spent more time on just 3 books?

He would have seen more results, and could share what he had learned with others in a meaningful way.

How do you go about actually mastering something? How do you go about choosing a book, studying the information and applying what you learned? First, always have your end result and what you're working towards (like your goal to be the top performer in your company, publish your book, start your company, etc.) in mind. You need to have a clear vision. Second, you need to make sure you pick a book that is congruent with that vision. You could reach out to the people in your circle of influence, or a mentor, and ask for recommendations, or email people who know you well and are influential and ask them to recommend a book that is related to your end result. The most important thing is that you choose a book, program, online course, or seminar that is in alignment with your vision and goals. The information must drive you closer to your goals.

After you've chosen the right book, make sure when you're reading it you don't move on to the next chapter until you can teach the chapter you've just read. I suggest you underline, add notes, and use place markers of the information you want to implement. Then go back and read it again and try to teach it to somebody you know so you can share what you learned and to reinforce this new information. Only then do you move onto the next chapter. This is the way you study and how you master your mindset.

A lot of people just read books as fast as they can without learning or mastering anything. Before I figured out how mastery mindset worked, I read a lot of books too, but I didn't remember what I read and I certainly didn't consciously apply what I learned. Now that I take the time to master 3 to 5 books per year, I've really seen the difference in my income and business strategy.

Mastering new skills is not an option in today's business environment. You have to start mastering skills and concepts, or in this competitive world, you're going to be left behind. Change is fast and inevitable. It's not enough just to be smart; you have to always be willing to learn, grow and adapt. If you're not growing forward, you're falling behind. Let me offer you some tips on how to improve your mastery mindset and avoid overwhelm and overload.

Start small: Realize that you can't take on everything at once, and if you do, you'll get overwhelmed, or you'll be paralyzed. Instead, choose one or two skills to focus on at a time and break each skill down into manageable goals. So often we try to take on too much or try and learn a skill that is just too complex. We get frustrated and disappointed in ourselves. Don't try to implement too much too quickly. This is two-fold. You want to have time to track if the new skill you implement is working and you want to make sure you really understand each new skill. A better way to stay motivated is by breaking each skill into small manageable tasks.

You'll see some progress, you'll feel some momentum, and both will help you stick with the skill you are trying to master. In my business, what really helped me get to the top 1% of the highest performers in my company is that I focused on one skill until I mastered it. By mastering each skill, one at a time, I was able to progress and prosper more quickly and easily. While everybody else was focusing on grasping a ton of skills at once, and not succeeding, I stuck with one skill at a time and it really paid off.

The third step in mastering is to take time to reflect along the way. To move from experimentation to mastery, you need to reflect on what you're learning. Otherwise, it simply won't stick. Talking about your progress helps you get valuable feedback, keeps you accountable, and really cements the new information. Like Jim Rohn said, "taking your past experience and investing it in your future success is a big key".

Another quick way to learn something new is to practice it, but even more important is to teach and share what you're learning and focusing on with your teams, your managers, your coworkers, your significant others, or even your customers. You'll quickly see a triple effect for mastering this new skill, as it will influence everyone around you to think differently and act differently, and you're going to the see the benefit of that in your progress and the progress of the company.

Be patient. Too often, we approach a new skill with the attitude that we have to nail it right away. The reality is it takes a long time to master a new skill or concept. Mastery of anything is not going to happen instantaneously. It can take two to six months, and sometimes up to a year to develop a new skill that's more complex, and ultimately, more valuable. Don't expect others around you to notice. It may take time for others to see and appreciate what you're learning, because people around you will only notice 10% of every 100% change you make. So stay focused, even when you don't get recognition from people around you.

Chapter III Action Steps

1. Write down your biggest goal you want to reach by the end of this year.

2. Pick 2 skills you need to master in order to achieve your biggest end of year goal.

3. Read, practice, and teach these 2 new skills until they become second nature to you.

You'll be amazed by the results you'll get when you practice this mastery mindset.

IV

Dropping Your Past and Transforming Your Future

For your results to change, you must change. In today's society, there are lots of young people who are so pumped, excited, ambitious and hungry, but they don't have the right strategies or resources to succeed. When I was younger and newer at sales, I would work 80 hours per week, but I wasn't achieving at the level I wanted, because I too didn't have the right information, the right people or the right mindset. In fact, I was broke and struggling. I see a lot of young people doing what I did – getting pumped up and working all the time, but not with a clear sense purpose and not really understanding what needs to change. I strongly believe the best way to predict someone's next six months of results is to look at their past six months.

If you want to determine if someone is an achiever, look at the results they've had in the past six months. If they don't have any, what makes you think they're going to achieve results in the next six months? Those achievers who are really crushing it out there are those that regularly track their results. And guess what? If they are crushing it in this part of the year, they'll be crushing it in the next. Most people don't think this way. In fact, most who struggle think more like this: "Thank goodness my last six months are over. I've been struggling, I'm stressed out, now I'm ready to crush it." But if you haven't made any changes, and you haven't seen any results, you aren't going to crush it. Period. That's why it's so important to create your circle of influence so you have accountability. When people join our Game Changer community, they make a big shift.

People in our community have actually ripped up their past script and have totally transformed their businesses by increasing productivity. By surrounding themselves with a new circle of like-minded people and ideas, they start thinking and behaving differently. They gain new strategies and new mindsets that are aligned with their bigger vision. Plus, many people in our Game Changers Community have already created success and are able to share how they achieved their results. Why am I telling you all this? I want you to understand that unless you make some big change, allow new information into your brain, and make some adjustments in the actions you're taking today, your next six months will be exactly the same as your last six months.

I know a guy who has been spinning in circles for months. He's not growing. And what's interesting is he thinks he doesn't need help and already knows everything. A big part of his spinning has to do with not trying new strategies or new ideas. If you're doing the same things over and over, and you're not trying new ideas or new strategies, you'll continually tread water and stay stuck where you are, just like the guy who thinks he knows everything already. When you read a book, or you talk to a mentor, or you reach out to somebody, they give you new information and a new perspective on your situation or business problem, and then you decide to either take action on it or not.

For example, I recently met with two successful entrepreneurs. Because of their success, they offered ideas that I hadn't thought about regarding expanding my business at a very high level. If I hadn't agreed to meet with them, I would be limiting my potential and miss some great opportunities for growth. If you're reading this book, I'm confident that you also want big growth and big results. My guess is that you are willing to do the work and reach out to people as well. Maybe you just don't know how to put all the puzzle pieces together or how to get started. By the end of this book, you'll have all the pieces and the action steps you need to be successful.

This is a great time to talk about activity. This is going to sound far too easy, but I assure you, it's very powerful! Simplify everything. Remember, I'm all about mastery not overload. I want clear, simple information and action steps. Here's a powerful exercise you can do right now so you can really start really clear, guided and smart action. Don't skip this part. Take out a piece of paper or start a new word doc and do the following exercise: Write or type your top five goals for the year. If nothing else happens this year but these five things, would it be your best year ever? What five things have to happen for this to be your best year ever? Write or type your top five goals right now. Don't resist and don't self-edit. You can always adjust later, but the important thing is that you gain clarity around the top five.

Remember, reasons come first, results come second. So now that you have your top 5, you need to write or type your top ten reasons why you want to achieve those five goals. I want you to be fully focused here. If you choose to move on without doing this important exercise, I encourage you to at least write the steps down and complete it soon.

After you write down your top ten reasons, review them. Are all of them really good reasons? Let me share a story with you first and then we'll go back to your reasons. One of the entrepreneurs in our program is helping pay his mother's bills. She's a single mother raising four kids. Although she was trying, she just wasn't making enough money to cover the bills. He's now making $4,000 - $5,000 a month because of the program, and his compelling internal reason to make money – to help his family. His reason to earn money is so strong that he's not going to let himself sleep in because he has a family to protect. Having strong reasons is important because they encourage motivation, and when you are motivated, you take action. Now, let's go back and review your ten reasons. Which of these reasons are really going to keep you motivated in action? Circle those reasons.

The next step is really about getting clear on what's working and what isn't. Let's begin with what you need to start doing which you aren't already doing, but know you need to be doing to reach your top five goals. Use your reasons as fuel. Figure out what you need to do. For example, maybe you need to start waking up earlier to study. Or maybe you need to start reaching out to higher level people or join a community that helps improve your mindset, your results, your time management, or your productivity skills. Maybe you need to start eating healthier. So if you had a goal of learning new business strategies for your business growth, you could start reading 10 pages a day from a purposeful book. What you need to make sure of is that the actions you choose to take are congruent with your top five goals.

The next thing you are going to do will be a bit more challenging. I want you to write down everything that you need to stop doing that is holding you back from achieving your goals. This is a pretty big one, right?

You need to stop making excuses, or you need to stop going out late. Maybe you need to stop partying on the weekends if you aren't getting the results you really want. These are things that might hurt in the moment, but the payoff is tremendous. What are you going to stop doing?

Finally, give yourself credit where credit is due. What are you going to continue to do that you're already doing well and that's serving you? What are you going to continue doing? If you are already waking up early to exercise, great! Write "continue" next to that. Or maybe you are already listening to great podcasts that teach you about strategy, leadership or sales. Keep doing that.

Congratulations for following through on that painful, but necessary exercise. Once you have your goals, reasons and action steps written down, you'll need to make a commitment to look at this list daily for one week. And I want you to be honest with yourself. Are you really starting what you committed to start? Are you stopping what you need to stop? And are you continuing with things that are serving you well? The only way to reach those top goals for the year is by reviewing your list every couple of weeks and monitoring your progress honestly. If you've taken the time to write all of these commitments down, but never look at it again, you will come back in a month and go "Oh crap. Now I'm doing the same thing I've been doing." This is something you have to consistently do and work at making this list better by reviewing and tweaking regularly. If you are aware of your commitments and your reasons, you have a way better shot at hitting those top five goals. Most people's New Year's Resolutions are out the door by the first week of February. If you asked them what their New Year's Resolutions were, most can't remember. In order to achieve your goals, the reality is you need this list and you need to constantly revisit it in order to stay on track and stay motivated. And don't do this once every five months. Do this once per month. As you continue to improve the level of your awareness, your intention and really how you're going about your days, weeks, months, you'll begin to see what is missing so that you can reach your goals.

I see some patterns where people tend to fail when using their lists. Some people continue to get tripped up by a specific issue or a specific struggle. They get overloaded with different information and they take too many opinions. They set a goal, while a friend of theirs will have a different goal. Suddenly, they'll switch goals to match their friend's goal, even if this goal has no real meaning for them. It's that bandwagon thing. The problem is they are never actually focused on the goals that are specific to them, and, guess what? They continue to struggle and seek more information. They are never actually focused consistently on moving towards one goal, which leads to little or no progress.

Another pattern I see that trips people up is scattered learning objectives. They will read a book on leadership, then they will watch a video on mental toughness, then they will read an article on money. When you put so much information in your head, it's very hard to pinpoint, take action, and see improvement. It's best to reverse engineer and figure out exactly what your goals are, and then work out which one or two skills you need to master to reach your goals. Stick with those two skills, implement and measure your progress weekly. This is so much more effective than trying to learn everything at once.

The biggest pattern I see that really trips people up is focusing too much on their feelings. "I don't feel like it." I call this "spur of the moment emotional train." You'll never find a six-figure earner or a millionaire, who's a "feeling" guy. Of course, they are passionate and have feelings, but they don't rely on their feelings when it comes to their commitments. You'll never find someone who is successful who bases things on their emotions or feelings. If you are scattered, focus primarily on your feelings, and lack consistent action, no matter how much you take in, you won't succeed. The way to combat this is to shift your circle of influence to include people who can hold you to higher standards and hold you accountable versus let you off the hook. Stop hanging around people who don't hold you to the fire. I know you don't want to be average and I know you want to succeed. Stay focused, take smart, guided action and don't let your emotions determine what you do or don't do when it comes to your commitments. Most people spend the first half of their life saying, "Oh I'm too young to be successful." Then sadly spend the second half saying, "Oh I'm too old to be successful." Age has nothing to do with it. Your mindset, however, does.

If you put off doing the exercise in this chapter, I encourage you to take the time now to complete it before moving ahead.

V

The 6 "Musts" to Extreme Achievement

This chapter makes a big promise. I'm going to give you the six musts to accomplish extreme achievement, or as I call them, the six C's. These six C's keep you from doing dumb stuff that doesn't help your business. Here's the truth: We all do dumb things in business and in our lives that keep us from moving forward and realizing our dreams. I'm no different. I had to learn the hard way to stop doing dumb stuff.

When I was broke and stressed, I was blaming my company, the economy, my lack of resources, and my location. I didn't have the proper training or the right habits in place to create wealth. I came to realize that my focus was jaded, and I needed to change my attitude and my intentions first before I could achieve my goals. The moment I got clear on this is the moment my life shifted from complexity and stress to simplicity and motivation. You can do the same by using these six C's. I'll touch on all six musts here simply. Then in the next couple of chapters, I'll dive into each one in detail and give actionable, tangible steps for you to follow that will increase your results at a pretty big level. If you continue to master these, it's guaranteed the six figures will come.

The first must to extreme achievement is clarity. Clarity is ultimate power. If you want results you've never gotten, you've got to get one hundred percent clear on what you want. I wasn't taking full responsibility, but when I did, I started to see a huge change in my results. I got crystal clear on what I wanted. I was sick of being broke and stressed. I was also frustrated with letting people down, including myself. Something amazing happens when you gain clarity. Confidence follows.

The second must is confidence. If you don't have confidence, you're always going to find a way to lose. You know those people for whom something good happens, but they go back to being average, or they get money and they go back to being broke? It's because their confidence level isn't matching up with what they've accomplished so they can't keep the momentum of the win going. Everything that you're accomplishing right now is based on the confidence you have in yourself and your ability to make things happen.

The bigger the goal you have, the bigger the challenges you'll face. The moment you set bigger goals, obstacles will appear, and they show up to really test your character and faith to see if you're serious about reaching those goals. If there were no challenges, it would be easy and everyone would be living their dreams. This is why I make sure that every choice I make serves to bolster my confidence because I've learned that with every decision, I am either helping or hurting my confidence. There's no in-between. If you think about people who are accomplishing more, they're simply doing so because they are continuing to make the choices that are harder in the moment, and they're choosing growth over staying the same.

Here are a few examples of how your decisions drive your confidence. If tomorrow you choose to sleep in instead of waking up early, does your confidence go up or down? If you choose to party versus study, you feel good in the moment but what happens the next day? You're going to be stressed about the test or the class that's coming up. And obviously, this will decrease your confidence. Or let's say you have a chance to go to a "self help" seminar, or go to the beach. Now, in the moment, you'll want to choose the beach because let's face it, relaxing or playing at the beach is more fun, but that seminar may offer the exact information you need to bring about your freedom to enjoy the beach more regularly. Serious and committed entrepreneurs think about what's better long term, and are disciplined enough to delay gratification over gaining instant satisfaction.

Once I started basing my decisions on my future and my vision as opposed to my current feelings, my confidence skyrocketed. As John C. Maxwell says, "It's not what you do when you're at the top that makes you a great leader. It's what you do when you're at the bottom that determines your leadership ability." When I was at the bottom, I started making decisions that would move me forward in my goals. I started reading and investing in myself. I started going to seminars and reaching out to people who could mentor me, and my confidence and skillset grew tremendously.

Once your confidence increases, you have to reevaluate your circle of influence. If your confidence grows, but you're still hanging out with the same people, you're not going to have the right steps or the right guidance to continue growing. Therefore, I reevaluated my circle of influence. Jim Rohn said it best, "Who you associate with is who you become," and I didn't want to be like the people I was around when I was broke and stressed. To be completely blunt with you, everyone I was around was struggling, and some of them were okay with mediocrity, but I wasn't. And I don't think anybody reading this is happy with mediocrity, or you wouldn't have chosen this book.

I started reaching out to those who had the success I wanted to achieve. It's been the biggest key to my success. When I was at my lowest point, financially and personally, I came across some powerful words that changed everything for me: "If you want to be a millionaire, talk to billionaires, because you'll get there quicker." I realized I wasn't achieving what I wanted because I wasn't surrounded by people who could help me. I knew then that I needed to reach out to the top performers in my industry so I could learn, grow and achieve. I made the decision that day to reach out and spend time with those people. Once I changed my circle of influence, I started shifting my standards. These top performers gave me actions to take, they shared the mistakes they made and told me what I should avoid, and all of a sudden I had a clear path. That's why the third must is circle of influence.

The fourth must is consistent energy and motivation. Once your circle of influence shifts, and your confidence is up, it's not sustainable unless you really focus on consistency. I noticed other entrepreneurs around me getting pumped up about new goals and achievements but they'd never stay consistent. Or they'd get pumped up and build some momentum and then take a vacation. They get super excited and do well, but then they'd take three days off and their momentum and motivation would wane. I realized that the key to success included consistency, so I made a commitment to follow through, and that gave me the competitive edge.

I caution you here a bit. Lack of consistency is subtle, but it's the biggest stealer of your dreams and desires. I consistently improved my mindset, my emotional intelligence, my perspective, and really how I viewed myself, not just when I felt like it, but consistently. This brought a very powerful force of momentum in my business and personal life. Nothing brings more excitement and confidence than progressing towards your goals.

The fifth must is creating results rituals. Once I learned where my results were coming from, I created rituals that moved my business forward. Every single week, I made sure I did the high value activities that I knew were creating results.

It's not the hours you work, but the work you put into those hours.

I was more intentional with my actions, which was something I learned from the people in my circle. I started organizing and scheduling my day around my priorities and visions, regardless of how I felt.

Once you have clarity, consistency, the right circle of influence, and your results rituals, the last must is continual growth and learning. To reach new heights in your life and business, you must be willing to grow and learn continuously in order to be the best at what you do. 95% of people aren't performing at a higher level because they aren't committed to continued learning. Once they reach a certain level, they stop performing or they stop growing. When you focus on growth and reaching out to even higher-level people, you'll stay motivated. So my learning didn't stop when I became successful. That's when it actually started.

If you consistently reach out to people who are playing the game at a higher level, you build your character, you develop more skills, and you continue to add more value to others. New concepts and habits that were hard for you before are suddenly second nature now. You learn about leverage and scale your growth with partnerships and sponsorships, and you'll see clearly how to take your business to exciting new levels.

Now you have the six musts to extreme achievement. Let's go in depth with each of these so you can reach your first six figures and beyond.

VI

Why Your Money Mindset Matters

This next topic is something that is very important to us (vital, really) but at times can be quite a controversial subject: MONEY. Is money important? How do you track money? How do you earn it? Let's discuss money and how you actually should handle it as an entrepreneur.

My view on money has certainly changed over the years. I was always excited about having money when I was younger, but the way I view money is different now. I base my view of money on facts and statistics rather than how people think or feel about money. If I asked all of my members if they wanted to be financially free when they were 65, how many do you think would say yes? All of them, of course. But if you fast forward to 65, here's the real statistics, reported by the Social Security board in Washington, D.C.: **69% of Americans over 65 are dependent on relatives, friends, or charities for income, 29% are still working and 2% are financially independent**.

No one plans on being dependent on others financially at 65 or older. Most seniors who are struggling today didn't plan to need help. They thought, like most of us, that they would be fine because they had so many years to earn money. But, somehow in those years, something goes wrong. Here's the truth: You have to plan today for your retirement and you have to invest in yourself now. This all starts with investing in your mindset and surrounding yourself with people who are financially stable instead of struggling. You'll never meet a successful, fulfilled person who doesn't invest in themselves.

Money, in and of itself, doesn't make you happy--on the other hand, it doesn't make you sad either. Zig Ziglar said it best: "Money isn't everything, but it is right up there with oxygen." Money buys you the freedom to watch your kids grow up, to pursue your craziest dreams, to make a difference in the world, to build and strengthen relationships, and to do what you love. Money is simply a tool and how you think about money affects how you earn it, how you spend it and how much you can make. You have to get your mindset around money corrected so you clear the path for money to flow to you consistently.

One of my mentors I grew up listening to was mentored by the Dalai Lama. She was at a seminar when she was younger and there was a very well known and successful presenter on stage. He was a businessman, speaker, and author, and he had an audience of thousands of people. He said he had $3000 in cash in his pocket, and he took it out and he started counting it. He said, "I love money. Oh, money's amazing! Oh I love it." He just kept saying, "I love money. Money's my best friend. I'm attracting money to me," while he continued to count the bills. Then he asked the audience, "If any of you guys just got mad or disgusted, you're repelling money away from you, and I guarantee you're close to broke." The reality is most people see money as bad or evil, and they tend to have a negative reaction when other people have money. Many times, people resist money because they're afraid people will see them as greedy. What they don't realize is that having money can help you do amazing things.

The first mindset flip is to love money and to invite and attract money to you. The reason that the successful presenter had money and wealth was because he was open to receiving it. He didn't let other people's feelings affect how he viewed money and neither should you.

Money helps you inspire other people, build a thriving business, and have more time with friends and family. People who have a good amount of money (AKA being financially free) are happier and live more fulfilling lives, not because of the money, but because of what the money offers to their lives.

You must have a conscious perspective flip that money is good. Realize that usually, with people who have money versus people who don't, it doesn't mean they got some special break or that they're lucky. They just attracted it, and worked harder and smarter on the right opportunities. In order to attract money, you have to see money and what it offers you and others as good. You have to welcome it and be excited about it. Surround yourself with people who have that similar mindset as well. If you add up the income of the five people you hang around the most, and then you divide it by 5, that's what your income is going to be on average. Just remain aware of your feelings and thoughts about money and how those people you surround yourself with view money.

Here are some tips to help encourage a healthy money mindset. When you talk about wealth and money, make sure you define what that means to you. Most people don't know why they want more money. They have associated money with the answer. But it isn't the money that will solve their problems – it's what the money can do for their lives and businesses that changes everything. You first have to define wealth in these terms in order to change how money comes to you.

For example, for some people wealth could be flexibility. Wealth could be freedom. Wealth could be peace of mind, health, or a great family. You have to organize your priorities based on your values and what you want. When people ask me about wealth, I ask them to tell me what wealth means to them. For some people, wealth means making forty or fifty thousand a year. To others, it means having freedom, flexibility, working for themselves, having peace of mind, or being with family. You have to define what wealth means to you. What will the money you make do to improve your life? For me, wealth is really freedom and a comfortable lifestyle that's healthy and energized. You have to define wealth before you can figure out what kind of income you want to make.

If you really want to build wealth, you have to build a wealth of intelligent knowledge first, and you have to study the wealthy. Get addicted and excited about saving, not spending -- unless you're investing in yourself, business, or assets that make money work for you. Live like a broke college student when you're younger. Even if you make money, live like you're broke, but think like a millionaire until your money catches up to your mindset.

Two things to help attract money and create income are your mindset and creating a higher impact. Impact more people with what you do and you'll create more wealth for yourself. You have to understand that you will always get paid for bringing value to the marketplace, and if you're not very valuable, you won't make much money. This was an eye opener for me because I realized I wasn't doing much to become more valuable, and I wasn't making much money either. People tend to complain about the economy, their job, the lack of income, but they aren't doing much to improve their skills and the harsh reality is...you're paid exactly what you're worth.

If somebody's making eight dollars per hour that is the value they're bringing to the marketplace. Why would somebody make $500 an hour but somebody else make only $8 an hour? One is more valuable to the marketplace than the other. If you're not very valuable, you're not going to make much money. The quicker you understand this, the quicker you're going to advance in the new economy.

Learn to work harder on yourself than you do on your job. If you work hard on your job, you'll make a living, but if you work hard on yourself, you'll make a fortune. Focus on doing what you're the best at, but predetermine and make sure that creates income. Figure out how to be the best in the world at what you are best at, and add more value than anybody else. Trust me, the money will come.

Chapter VI Action Steps:

1. Write down all of your feelings and thoughts about money. Cross out all negative statements.

2. Write down counter positive statements about money. Circle each one.

3. Write down all the gifts money will bring to your life and business.

4. Write or type your positive statements about money and what having wealth means to you. Post in a prominent area and make a copy to carry with you at all times. Refer to these when those old negative thoughts and feelings about money surface. Make a conscious effort to change your money mindset.

VII

Seven Trends of Young Millionaires

If you pay a mortgage, pay rent, or you have a lease on an office, quit complaining about the cost of it. I was just at an office in New York City that was $28,000 a month for rent. It's an amazing company. I guarantee the owner of the company wasn't complaining about the rent.

There are some 16, 17, and 18-year-old millionaires who can afford 28 grand a month for rent and not even sweat. And there are some 40 and 50 year olds who can't pay their mortgages. It's just crazy how our world works and what's going on right now.

The reason I'm talking about the trends of young millionaires is because I want to create young millionaires. The world needs millionaires. Millionaires provide jobs and inspire people. I've studied a lot of millionaires. I made my first million before turning 27, so I know exactly what it takes, and I love teaching young entrepreneurs like you how to create your first million.

One of my mentors, Jordan Wirsz, made his first million when he was only 21 years old. Just close your eyes and imagine your checking account having one million dollars in it from your efforts and hard work. How much confidence would you have? How much impact could you create? What kind of businesses could you build? That's a pretty amazing feeling, isn't it? I want you to start thinking like a millionaire. Millionaires are no different than you. It's their habits and perspective that separates them from the rest of society. There are certain trends that all millionaires have in common.

A lot of people don't even go for a million because they've heard so many people validate why you shouldn't go after money. They'll say things like I don't care about money, millionaires aren't happy, or I don't need that much money. I'm sure you could think of about 100 other validations, right? But I want you to realize that it's a good thing to want to become a millionaire. It's a good thing to want to make more money.

Don't let those people, especially those who are in debt, talk you out of becoming a millionaire. You don't make a million by accident or by luck. Even if you win the lottery, you'll most likely be broke in less than two years (The National Endowment for Financial Education cites research estimating that 70 percent of people who suddenly receive a large sum of money will lose it within a few years) BECAUSE they didn't earn it, so their money mindset was capped at their previous income.

The number one thing millionaires have in common is urgency. Every successful person has a sense of urgency. They feel like they don't have time to waste and they never stop growing or learning. The best companies on the planet love young talent and those who have purpose and a sense of urgency. Google is hiring more teenagers than college students. If you want to get your dream job, you need to show you have urgency. What does having a sense of urgency really mean? It means you realize that now matters more than any other time in your life. The "someday" mentality is killing many people's goals and ambitions. I know people who have been in the same company for years, and they are not growing or really taking advantage of their opportunities, and they're wondering why they don't get paid more. People always say, "I have 20 years of experience", but the reality is they only have one year of experience repeated for 20 years. If you do the same work you've always done, you'll get the same pay you've always gotten. You must have a sense of urgency if you're serious about your first million, and if you're serious about success.

I was recently in Hawaii because an owner of a large company asked me to come and talk to his sales staff in order to motivate them. Hawaii has a pretty laid back culture, but I can motivate anybody so I jumped at the opportunity. The reality was that many were just really laid back and had no sense of urgency, but there were many people in the company who didn't have the job they wanted, the money they wanted, and they weren't fulfilled. The most interesting part about this is that none of those people had a sense of urgency. They didn't understand that by not having a real urgency to make more, do more or be more was exactly what was keeping them stuck in their positions and their salaries.

The second trend of young millionaires is they all have an elevated influence. Behind every young millionaire, you're going to find an educated and very wise mentor. I have yet to meet, speak to, or study **any** millionaires or billionaires who don't have mentors to guide them, challenge them, and really push then to think bigger. You have to have someone guide you if you want to be successful. Successful people inherently understand that it's impossible to grow, learn, or become the person necessary to reach the million-dollar mark without having an exceptional mentor network behind you. Success really rises and falls based on who you associate with, so make sure you stay aware of who surrounds you.

Jordan, one of my mentors, told me you can systemize a lot of things, but you can't systemize time, so make sure you're spending your time with the right people. He also said you can't systemize relationships, so make sure you build the right ones. I see companies trying to automate and systemize everything and they're failing because they're trying to systemize relationships with people, but that simply doesn't work. Millionaires understand that they can't systemize time or relationships, so they're spending both really wisely, whether they're 14, 26 or 60 years old. So the third trend of successful millionaires is they manage their time and their relationships wisely.

The fourth trend of young millionaires is they maximize their strengths. As Gary Vaynerchuk says, "I suck at 99% of stuff I do, but I go all out on that 1% I'm good at." We're conditioned by our teachers, our peers, our parents, uneducated coaches, and everyone who gives advice to work on and strengthen our weaknesses. This is very bad advice. All millionaires focus 100% on what they're best at and they delegate the rest to others. They find people around them who are good at what they are not. They naturally learn to surround themselves with people who complement their weaknesses. You'll never get wealthy focusing on things that you suck at, so focus your attention and your time on your strengths. Use them as an advantage and find others to do the stuff you don't like or you're not good at. This will be a game changer for your life and your business.

Think about what you can become the best at. What's your one strength you can focus on? Once you master one strength and start producing real results, you can move on to mastering another strength. The key is to focus on maximizing your very best strengths.

The fifth trend is young entrepreneurs never trade time for money. They quickly realize they'll never become wealthy trading time for money, and you won't either. It's okay for a while, but at some point, you have to focus on scaling and leveraging your business. One of the main reasons entrepreneurship, direct sales, internet businesses, coaching, speaking, and network marketing are growing exponentially right now is because you don't have to trade time for money. It's not easy, and it takes some risk, but if you see past the risks and focus on the rewards, you'll see some pretty amazing results.

I know 18 and 19-year-olds who are making $20,000 a month by leveraging their businesses. Focus on the power of leverage and building teams to create consistent income without trading time for money and you'll be amazed at what you can accomplish. One of the best books I've ever read, is by MJ DeMarco, called, *The Millionaire Fast Lane* it's a true game changer in understanding exponential monetary growth. For example, he encourages investment properties, membership sites, building a brand, joint partnerships, affiliate marketing programs, products, speaking engagements as ways to earn income without trading your time. Take a moment to analyze if you're maximizing your time now and if you're trading time for money. Make sure it's an intelligent trade. If you're at the mall working or at the clothing store trading your time for $12 an hour, that's not an intelligent use of your time.

Now, your parents may think this is the only way to earn a living or make money because they didn't have the luxury of today's economy and global possibilities when they were younger. You are in a different economic and technological time. You have the choice in how you earn your money, how you use your time and how you live your life. Don't get down on your parents though or expect them to understand. They were simply raised in different times with different societal expectations. Think about your time and how you want to spend it. Be open to the possibility of creating an online program, community, or product that can earn income while you sleep. It is more than possible.

Millionaires become millionaires because they've added more value to the marketplace than anybody else, and they understand the power of leveraging and scaling their businesses. And the sixth trend of these millionaires is they could care less what anybody else thinks about them. They are neither concerned with being liked nor concerned with getting approval. You have to drop the need to be liked if you want an extraordinary life. People who care what others think about them will always be limited by other people's opinions. Millionaires take very few opinions and are extremely thick skinned. When you pursue greatness, you can't expect people to support you all the time because you're representing the strength, courage, passion, and vision that oftentimes they don't have.

As Steve Jobs said, "your time is limited so don't ever waste it living someone else's life". Young millionaires trust in their vision and have a lot of confidence in what they do even when everyone else doubts them. I challenge you to be fearless with your vision regardless of what people say. Stay focused on what you want. A huge key to your success is not worrying about what others think about you.

The seventh trend is that entrepreneurs are producers first, consumers second. Most people are consumers first and consumers second. They don't produce anything. MJ DeMarco talks about this in *The Millionaire Fast Lane.* Instead of buying products on TV, sell products. Instead of digging for gold, sell shovels. Instead of taking a class, offer one. Instead of borrowing money, lend it. Instead of taking a job, hire for jobs. Instead of taking a mortgage, hold the mortgage. Break free from consumption, switch sides and go through the world as a producer not a consumer. To consume richly, you must produce richly first if you're really serious about becoming wealthy.

Unfortunately, most people have it backwards: all consumption and no production. Producers get rich and consumers get poor. Focus on being a producer first, and you'll build and attract more wealth. Entrepreneurs focus on building something bigger than them, are consistently on purpose and are always producing instead of buying, buying, buying. They're actually producing products and services that solve people's specific problems.

Now you have the seven trends of young millionaires. If you're serious about being a millionaire or even making your first six figures, become more intentional and start applying these seven trends to your life.

Chapter VII Action Steps:

1. Write or type the seven trends of young millionaires.

2. Ask yourself if you're following these trends every single day. It's important to apply these trends NOW.

3. Instead of focusing on what you can buy, brainstorm ideas for producing something you can sell to solve people's problems and make an impact on people's lives.

VIII

If Winning Was Easy, Losers Would Do It

Let's talk about being a winner and the things that winners do that others don't. In today's economy, we need more people going for greatness versus staying comfortable. A winner is defined as someone who is always reaching new heights and new ambitions. They're not easily satisfied. They don't stop until they fulfill their purpose and do what they were born to do while serving as many people as possible in the process.

Winners are always passionate about what they do and they get results at the same time. They make sure that what they're good at and what they're passionate about creates a sustainable income and an amazing living for them. You have to find some things that you're really good at and passionate about because you get results when you are passionate about the work you do.

Winners focus on the inside, not the outside. They focus on their inner game and their inner game is a reflection of their outer game. All winners consistently reflect on themselves. Winners are extremely competitive, but who do you think they're competitive with the most? Themselves. The only person who could stop Michael Jordan was Michael Jordan. The only person who can stop LeBron James is LeBron James. Winners are always focused on being better than they were the day before, the week before, the month before. They know there's always room for improvement.

I am coaching a young lady to help her get to the number one spot in the company I used to work for. She's just shy of the number one position. She came to me because she was frustrated with her results. She kept talking about the guy who was ahead of her. I asked her how she did this week versus last week. She fumbled for an answer. I told her all she needed to focus on was the progress she was making and what she could tweak the following week to get even better results. This one shift really changed her perspective and helped her focus on what she could control. Now she's crushing it because she's focusing on her specific goals and on being better every week.

That's what winners do--they concentrate on getting better. And winners love when people doubt them because they use that as ammunition instead of getting frustrated or discouraged. Here's an example: Michael Jordan wasn't playing too well defensively. He had an amazing offensive game, was MVP, and was the scoring leader of the NBA. But everyone said he couldn't play defense. I don't know if you're a sports fan, but the next year he was defensive player of the year! That's the type of mindset winners have.

You're not too good to learn from someone younger than you. I never let age get in the way of my opinions, and because of this I've learned from many people who were younger than me. And I'm not the only one who keeps an open mind when it comes to learning lessons. I was talking to the assistant coach for the Los Angeles Clippers and he shared a great story about Kobe Bryant. Kobe saw a high school all-star game and he noticed a particular move that a high school kid who using in that game. He went home and started to practice the move. A friend noticed Kobe practicing the same move over and over and he asked Kobe what he was doing. Kobe explained that he needed to practice this new move he saw. And his friend asked, "How long are you going to practice for?" Kobe responded, "Until it's perfected." How inspiring is that? There's a reason why he's Kobe, and most people who don't know anyone in sports will know Kobe's name because he's such an incredible player. It's because he does the unexpected and he does the extra work. Winners focus on something they want to improve on until it's mastered as opposed to giving up when it gets too hard.

Winners do the un-required work. What are you doing that's un-required? A lot of people do just enough to get by. Even if they're in sports, they do what everyone else does. They think their athleticism will take them to the next level, but there's only so much your athleticism can do. In the same way, there's only so much your skills can do in business, unless you're doing the un-required work. I encourage you to think about what you can do that no one else is doing in your industry or in your company, and do the un-required work to master that one aspect. Everybody wakes up early these days. Everybody's on personal growth these days. What are you doing that's un-required? What seminars are you going to? What programs are you joining? Who are you reaching out to? What are you doing that goes beyond what everyone else is doing?

Winners also persist on their path to success and use all failure as motivation. They have such a strong will to be the best and to win, they continue to persevere. Nothing gets in their way.

Furthermore, winners' perspective of their 24 hours is a lot different than the majority's perspective of 24 hours. This one shift changes everything. Time is, of course, a reality of life. You can't get it back. It's really the great equalizer. A lot of people feel like they have all the time in the world, but in many ways, whether you're living an amazing life or have a thriving business, your success or lack thereof has nothing to do with needing more time. Everything breaks down to how you manage your time. Successful people, the winners, always try to squeeze the most out of each day. They get in as much as they can so when their head hits the pillow, they're proud of what they accomplished that day. They didn't just get through the day; they got a lot from the day.

I know someone who's working a comfortable job, making about $1600 a week and he doesn't like it at all. He says, "I'm working 50 hours a week. I have no time to work on my other business and I have all of these ideas for this business I want to work on." So I asked him what time he wakes up. "Oh, like 7," he says. I told him if you want your business bad enough, you'll wake up at 5 a.m. If you really want to be a winner and you want to achieve greatness, you can't use having another job as an excuse not to work on your business.

It's not only what you do in those 8 hours that counts, but what you're willing to do in the after-hours that makes you successful. Everybody works 40 to 50 hours per week, whether you're a construction worker, an entrepreneur, a teacher, or a garbage man.

You want extreme success? The Michael Jordan, the Phil Ivey or the Tiger Woods kind of success? You've got to work the extra hours and show up day in and day out. If you want to get the most out of life and build a legacy, you have to put in the work every day to be a winner in this economy. Show up and take the time to perfect your skills.

Chapter VIII Action Steps:

1. Pay attention to how you spend your days over the next week.

2. Go beyond expectations and do the un-required work for just one day this week and reflect on how that feels.

3. Make a commitment to master one new skill.

IX

If You Want To Change The Game, Change Your Value

One of the biggest breakthroughs I've had came from what I experienced when I made the simple decision to increase my value. You can take what I share in this chapter and use it right away to increase your value and your income by at least ten percent. My income tripled by changing only this one thing: my value.

Before I changed my value, I was working a lot and not getting the results I wanted. Then I started getting better at time management, so I was working less and working smarter, but I still wasn't making the income I wanted. I had already learned from personal experience that when I changed my perspective, I created immediate positive shifts in my life and my business. So I knew that my perspective had to change again.

One of the greatest philosophers and mentors I've ever studied was Jim Rohn. He had an amazing impact on my upbringing and my success in business. If you understand this philosophy of Jim's and implement it into your life, you'll develop a big advantage over those who don't. "You get paid for bringing value to the marketplace, and if you're not very valuable, you don't make much money."

This was an eye opener for me because I realized I wasn't doing much to become more valuable, and obviously, I wasn't making much money. People tend to complain about the economy, their job, the government, and their lack of income, but yet they aren't doing much to improve their value or skills to increase their earning potential or get a better job. That's why very few people in our society are financially free and live amazing lives. One in three people still believe their best chance of becoming wealthy is by winning the lottery, despite the overwhelming statistics to the contrary.

Most people expect to make more money at a job simply because they've stayed at a job over a long period of time. The number of years at a specific occupation does not increase the value of the job being done. It doesn't matter if you've been there ten, twenty or thirty years. In most cases, staying at the same job doesn't increase the value of the employee either, especially if they perform the same kind of tasks over a long period of time. How often have you heard people say, "I have 20 years of experience, so I should get paid more." In actuality, unless that person has moved up in the company or taken on more responsibility, that person has only one year of experience repeated a thousand times. If you're not sharpening your skills or learning better tools, or constantly trying to improve yourself to become more valuable, more money will not come to you. Age isn't value.

Most employees want more money but are unwilling to do anything that delivers more value to the business or the customers. Jim Rohn said it perfectly, "Don't bring your needs to the marketplace; bring your skills." What he's saying is we get paid for the value we bring to other people's lives. Skills are valuable; needs are not. You might have a desperate need for money to pay medical bills or the mortgage, but unless you are adding value to your company or your clients, you'll never attract more wealth. The marketplace rewards value, not need. Focus on what you are offering and how you can improve and be the best, then money will flow easily and steadily.

Jim Rohn also said this, "If you don't feel well, tell your doctor, but not the marketplace because the marketplace is only interested in what you can do for it value wise." The fact that you're not doing well is just a lame excuse to the marketplace. It's not interested. It wants results and it wants value from you. So, if you need money, go to the bank, but not the marketplace. Don't ask for anything without offering something in return. And what does the marketplace want? Value in exchange for money.

Here's the secret: You need to learn to work harder on yourself than you do on your job. If you work hard at your job, you'll make a living, but if you work hard on yourself, you'll make a fortune. You don't need to work on the economy. You don't need to change your company. You don't need to change the government, your boss, or your circumstances. You just need to go to work on yourself because if you change, everything will change for you. Remember, you are the constant. You may change companies, you might change tactics, strategies, or mentors, but you are always the constant. I ask people this question when they're not doing well in business or at a company: Do you realize that when you leave this company, you're taking you with you? Wherever you go, you're there. If you want your outside circumstances to change, change from the inside first.

I've seen people change companies and in a couple months, the same thing happens to them again and they're actually surprised! They make the same excuses, blaming the company, the boss, and their managers without realizing the problem lies with them. It can't be four companies in a row, dude. Someone else in that company's succeeding, right? So, the reality is, wherever you are, you're there, so make sure you're being honest with yourself and what value you offer. Labor to become a better person every day and you will start becoming more valuable to yourself, your business or the company you work for now.

How do you bring value to the marketplace? By becoming better at everything you do. I used to tell my sales force their goal is to become irreplaceable and to become so good at what they do that people can't ignore them. People who choose to work at minimum wage jobs are very easily replaced because the work can be done by almost anyone, which is not very valuable to the marketplace. And nobody wants to feel replaceable, right? If you consistently build your character, your skills and increase your value, you will quickly advance in this game of economics. If you want to take it to the next level, you need to make growth a part of your daily agenda. Do something that increases the value you bring to your business, your work, your clients, your customers, and even your family, and you will start to see your income increase.

Simply put, if you're not happy with your current income level, it's not very complicated to change it. You simply need to offer more value to the marketplace, and in order to do that you need to follow a self-development plan that will enable you to put your skills, your habits, and your new disciplines to work to increase your value to the marketplace.

Is it possible to become twice as valuable to the marketplace? Is it possible to make double the money in the same amount of time? Yes. My first summer, I ran a sales office. I worked 80 hours a week and didn’t make much money. Five years later, I worked 20 to 25 hours a week and made six figures that summer. How did this happen for me? I became more intelligent, more valuable, more disciplined, gained new skills, and I was more aware as a leader. That's why the time I spent working went down but the income went way up. That shows you can sow your time and get anything you want because there's nothing more valuable than time invested wisely. Nothing is more priceless than your time. Never waste this precious gift. I take my time very seriously, and so should you.

We get paid for the value we offer, not the time we spend, so it's what you do with your time that really matters. Personally, I've never met a wealthy person who didn't value his time, and I've never met a poor person who did. Understand the value of time, because with time, anything can be accomplished if you spend it wisely.

Here are some ideas on how to spend your time to become more valuable:

Expertise: what you know.

Skills: what you do.

Productivity: what you get done.

Efficiency: how quickly you get things done.

Multiplication, Organization, and Duplication: how you get things done by means other than manual labor and by someone other than yourself.

Influence: what you can do to get others to get things done.

Relationships: who you know. Do your relationships challenge and stretch your thinking, your vision, personality and attitude?

These are areas you can focus on to get more valuable because there are really no limits to how much money you can make if you commit to growing at a higher level in this economy. This is the greatest time in human history for those who make the decision to become more valuable, who refuse to accept mediocrity and who take full responsibility for their economic well-being. Commit to becoming more valuable and you'll be rewarded by what happens to not only your income, but your influence and your lifestyle overall.

Chapter IX Action Steps:

1. Keep a journal of your time. In one column, record your time spent on income-producing activities and another column on time spent doing other activities.

2. Write down three income-producing activities you can start doing daily to maximize your income, your skills or your expertise.

3. Commit to those activities above and track your progress thirty days from today.

X

How To Build A World-Class Life

Many young entrepreneurs struggle with understanding how to build a world-class life. I want to help you create an exceptional lifestyle where there are no regrets, you're not trying to impress people, and you're thriving financially. You're doing what you love. You're getting results. You're getting paid for your efforts. There are very specific things you need to know before you can really live a world-class life.

You might be wondering, what exactly is a world-class life? The economy is changing like crazy right now, and one of the most important perspectives you can gain and understand is staying true to who you really are and to really feel alive and excited about everything that you do, which can be pretty difficult in a world filled with stereotypes and false judgments these days.

If you study successful people and those living their dreams, you'll find some commonality. They truly value and express who they are regardless of opinions or criticism. I've watched a lot of interviews of successful people and most, if not all of them, actually credit their success to staying confident in their core values, expressing their identity, and not conforming to anyone else's ideals or values. This is the only way to really express your genius and do well. You're going to run into people who doubt you because so many people are trying to fit in with the mainstream. They've given up on their goals, so they're going to try to put you down because they're not living the life they want.

The first key to living a world-class life is figuring out who you are and staying true to those core values. You can't change to fit the mold of society. When I was growing up, I was around so many different people and in different environments. I was a hyper and energetic kid. When I was really myself, I got ridiculed and got in trouble at school. I remember being told stuff like: "You need to be quiet! No, do it this way! Stop that! You can't be this energetic!" And it really made me resent school.

I don't feel school really gives students what they actually need to succeed. That's why most millionaires are dropouts. Now, I'm not saying school is bad. I mean, obviously, you need school for specific things; but because of the way it is currently structured, it doesn't lend itself to personal expression or creativity. Regardless of your environment, don't let other people's opinions drown out your real potential and your belief in yourself. You've got to embrace being different whether people like you or not. If you're being yourself, the right people will like the real you.

When I started doing podcasts, I knew they might turn off some people. I'm blunt and very direct. I don't want those people who are turned off by me to listen anyway. I want the people who can relate to me and who actually understand and get the value of what I teach. If you talk to anyone about me, it's likely that they will tell you I don't waste any time worrying about how people feel about me or what people think about me. It's not always easy, but I don't want to have everyone love a fake me.

You need to choose your values wisely and authentically. Be willing to deepen your sense of self. Create a personal philosophy for living.

Everyone is going to live life based on their own philosophy, period. If their philosophy tells them that when they're stressed out they must watch TV and forget about their problems, that's what they're going to do. If their philosophy tells them that when they're not making the money they want, they need to grind even harder, not sleep in, not do anything that's unproductive, and work harder until they get back to the success they want, that's what they're going to do. So you need to know your values and know what you care about the most. Doing this will increase your confidence and how people look at you, but most importantly, this will change how you feel about yourself. If you choose your values based on who you are and what you stand for, it won't matter what others think.

Jim Rohn is brilliant at this. He talks about how someone's philosophy determines their entire future, and how you sharpen your philosophy by experiences, by who you're around, by studying experts, by listening to podcasts, by joining programs that are congruent with your goals, and so on. I've taken a lot of my philosophies from the people I admire. People like Gary Vaynerchuk, Eric Thomas, Grant Cardone, and Isaac Tolpin, for example. There's a reason these people are successful. And studying them and what they are doing is a great way to build a world-class life.

Here's what I really want you to know. People's opinions are more about them than they are about you. Everyone sees the world through their own lens. This doesn't mean they're right, or they're better, or they're smarter than you. They're just different, and they have a different set of values, beliefs, and life experiences. For example, if I listened to half of my family's advice, I'd probably be broke right now or doing something I hate. That sounds so bad, but it's absolutely true. When I travel and see my family, I always have to remind myself that I'm living a different lifestyle than them. They believe, "Hey, you don't need to work. You need to relax a little bit. Stop working so hard." And I'm sure most people have experienced something similar, where your family gives you advice that doesn't relate to your values or goals. Their opinions may be valid or invalid, it doesn't matter. It's up to you to decide how outside opinions fit into your life. You have to be fiercely committed to your goals, your values, and your beliefs.

Trust your vision, even when everyone else doubts you. You have to drop the need to be liked if you want to create an amazing life. People who care what others think about them will always be limited by others' opinions. And when you pursue greatness, and when you pursue big things, you're going to get criticism. Grant Cardone says, "You need criticism, and you need haters before you get admiration." You're going to get people who doubt your vision, but if you stay strong and really continue to pursue it regardless of others, you'll eventually get to that milestone you've been defining for yourself. Most people, right when others start to doubt their vision, give up. And they're so close to that next peak or that next big accomplishment, but they cave-in to the doubts of others instead of staying true to their vision.

Keep a good circle of friends. The greatest support system in the world is a network of good friends. You can't be careless. You need friends, but you need to make sure that they hold you accountable and they make you better, versus simply letting you off the hook. Friends are those people who know everything about you and still like you anyway, right? So take care of them, and they'll take care of you. Inspire them, and they'll inspire you. There's nothing more valuable than your inner circle, so I would strongly recommend developing a very dynamic, powerful, and close inner circle.

No one can really guide you better than you guide yourself. So listening and learning from others has a lot of value, and the feedback from the right people is needed, but ultimately, your decisions are up to you.

Realize there are going to be naysayers, haters, people who doubt you, even people with strong opinions who appear against you. But only you know in your gut and in your heart what the right thing is for you. I have tremendous respect for people who are living lives that are congruent with who they are versus what others want them to be.

Chapter X Action Steps:

1. Write down or type your core values. What really matters most to you?

2. Review your values list and use one recent day. Ask yourself if what you spend your time doing reflects your values.

3. Develop your inner circle. Reach out to people who are achieving what you want to achieve. Look for groups to join in your area so you can network with like-minded people who want to grow and achieve.

XI

How To Build A World-Class Life [Part 2]

Earlier I was talking about how to build a world-class life. I talked about staying true to who you are, and how the only way to really build a world-class life is living your philosophy, choosing your values wisely, and not giving up on your vision just because others start to doubt it. We talked about how, really, the opinions people give are more about them than they are about you. And lastly, I discussed the power of a good circle of friends and a very close inner circle. Once you understand these principles, you can apply the next part of living a world-class life.

I was at an event in New York with my good friend Hal Elrod, and it was only for people who had revenue of $1 million or more a year who were invited to attend. It was extremely humbling to be surrounded by multi-millionaires. They talked about their challenges, frustrations, failures and their successes. What most fascinated me was how they are just like everybody else. They have the same insecurities, and the same things are going wrong in their lives that may be going wrong in yours. The only difference is they've put in more work than most people, or they've connected with the right people, or they have worked a little bit more intelligently to make that first million. But they have the same issues you do. Millionaires aren't perfect. They just continue working and grinding when most people stop.

Treat every person like they are extremely important. Why? Because they are. And when you respect others and find time to learn from them, you'll respect yourself at a higher level. A good personality is something that everyone can enjoy and draw energy from. When you're judging others, you're not really judging them. You're judging yourself. So most people don't treat others the way they ideally want to be treated. Treating others well will differentiate you from the crowd. Treat people like they are important and you'll be amazed at how they respond.

The next tip is what I learned from my mentor, Isaac Tolpin, founder of Choose Growth. It's called not fearing people. Stay fearless in everything. The reason most of us don't take risks, live on the edge, or push the envelope is the fear of what others will think of us. Even as I am about to take a risk or do something different, I catch myself thinking, "Oh, what are they going to think of me?" Then I remember Isaac's wise words. The more you fear people, the less effective you are as a leader. If you really want to live an exceptional, fun, and exciting life, you've got to drop the fear of what others think. Be aware of what your thoughts are when you are about to do something new or different.

If you start to question what other people will think about you, acknowledge that fear and do it anyway. Don't be afraid to speak up or take action because you're worried about what people might think or because you're worried that you'll look dumb. Know that you're not alone in that fear, but what will set you apart is your ability to take action in spite of the fear. And the sooner you press through those fears, the sooner you'll see massive success, feel more fulfilled, and experience bigger results as well. If you're in a leadership role and you manage a team, it's even more important because when they see you fearing people, they're going to subconsciously lose respect for you too.

I know this is tough. I've also had to get over fear. But when you meet legendary people, or you meet people who are extremely successful in their field, and you see how little they care about what others think, you'll realize how powerful moving through fear really is. You've got to be different. If you stay comfortable, never question bad ideas, worry you'll be criticized for speaking your mind, you're going to be just like everybody else. Sometimes you've got to speak out and share your thoughts. Some of the articles on RealVIPSuccess.com have some pretty controversial content, but it's what I truly, authentically believe. Once again, the right people are going to catch on and learn from what I share.

Value yourself and your choices. When you make a choice, and you made that choice based on your vision or based on what you think is right, go with it. Own the choices you make in your life because when you doubt yourself and your choices, others will too. When you believe in yourself, in time, others will believe in you as well. You've got to show massive confidence in your choices and what you stand for, regardless of whether others agree. I'm going to give you a million-dollar tip right here, and it's going to sound normal, but when you actually use it, it will make a world of difference in your success. I learned this from Mike Muriel, one of the top leaders in my previous company. One of the best things he taught me is that the person with the most confidence always wins. The person in a conversation who's more confident will win. I don't care if they're right or wrong. You have to have so much conviction and so much confidence in your decisions and what you say that the other person trusts you and they believe in your vision. It is, however, important that you are actually knowledgeable about what you are saying. The more you know and learn, the easier it is to speak with confidence.

If you talk to the billionaires like Elon Musk, Richard Branson, and Donald Trump, you'll see how confident they are in what they do and no one ever doubts them. If you take only one tip away from this chapter, having confidence in what you do and say is a great starting point towards building a world class life. Also, show that confidence whenever you're discussing your vision or talking about your goals. Value your choices and be confident in your decisions. You might be asking yourself OK, well how do I become more confident? Well confidence is impossible to teach because it has to be within you. You have to create confidence yourself by getting outside your comfort zone. You know that feeling when you're about to do something new like speak, perform or present in front of an audience, and your stomach is in knots? And you can't wait to get it over with? And then you do it. Then you go up on stage and just kill it. Do that over and over. I dedicated a whole chapter in my last book Six Months to Six Figures on confidence building.

Lastly, focus on gratitude. This will help you build a great life. No matter what your circumstances are, no matter what card life deals you, there's always something to be grateful for. Focus on gratitude. Because you'll find that all successful people practice gratitude. The best entrepreneurs, the best parents, the best athletes, and the best sales professionals all practice gratitude. So while most people are worried about the economic crisis, worried about watching the news, and worried about murders and killings, successful people focus their attention on all the good in their lives. They focus on things that actually add value to their lives. Stay focused on the good things versus the negativity and you'll start to feel your motivation, happiness, and energy increase.

Since it's such an important activity for a world-class life, I would like to discuss how to add more gratitude to your life. Every morning, write down three things you are grateful for today. One can be from your past, like your family, your health, or an opportunity you had. The second one can be one that is in the present, and the third can be what you are grateful for and appreciate in the future. I'm grateful for today. I'm going to be grateful for my team. I'm going to be grateful for the challenges that come my way in the future. Be grateful for things that you've had in your past, things you currently have, and things that are going to come your way. A journal is a great way to do this. Affirmations and visualization are also a great way. Being conscious about what you focus on multiplies and becomes your reality. So when something doesn't go your way, like being stuck in traffic, shift your focus and think about something you're grateful for instead. I had a gratitude card for a long time where I had what I was grateful for written down. So whenever I had a challenge, I thought about those 15 or 20 things I'm grateful for. Not even two minutes later, I'd be completely out of my funk. There are so many things to be grateful for every day that we completely take for granted unless we make a conscious effort to appreciate what we do have. And the funny thing about being grateful is the more grateful you are for what you have, the more you have to be grateful for.

Another way to express gratitude is to help someone in need. When you do that, you'll not only appreciate where you are, but you'll feel better because you're helping somebody else. You're doing something that's outside of yourself and it'll make you forget about your problems very quickly.

Chapter XI Action Steps:

1. Start a gratitude journal. Write down three things you are grateful for from the past, present and the future. Do this every day.

2. If you are having trouble feeling grateful on a daily basis, make a commitment to help someone in need. Volunteer at a shelter, donate school supplies to kids in need, or spend time at a senior center.

XII

Why Standards Matter And How To Raise Yours

Let's take a moment and talk about your standards. I try to hold everything to a really high standard. Why is this important? Why do you need that in your life? I didn't always have them, but your standards usually rise with the circle of influence you have. One of the downfalls in our current society is so many people have given up on their goals, their dreams, and their true passions. Just to be blunt, it seems like giving up is the common theme today (even the divorce rate is over 50%). We've been conditioned to take what we get versus fight for what we want. And sadly, most people have lowered their standards. That's why I want you to raise your standards – so you can have more, be more and do more. Your standards play a big part in your current situation, your performance, your happiness, and creating the life of your dreams.

I raised my standards because everybody around me was raising their standards, and I realized I wasn't giving my all. Once my standards rose, everything else in my life started to rise as well. You get exactly what you tolerate, and life's going to organize results around the standards that you set for yourself.

There are five steps in raising your standards. The first step is you have to pick two or three areas of your life that you want to improve. In this instance, what I mean by standards is what you tolerate and how people treat you. Here's an example. If you raise your standards in one particular area, you'll raise that area of your life. If you tolerate being disrespected, you'll always be disrespected. If you tolerate being overworked and underpaid, you'll continue to be overworked and underpaid. If you tolerate being overweight, you'll always be overweight. If you tolerate being broke, you'll always be broke. So think about the areas you want to improve: happiness, income, your relationship with your spouse, how your boss treats you, your health and energy. That's what I mean. Say you decide to raise your standards income-wise. Maybe you're sick of not having the money you want. Then make the commitment to raise your standards in this area. Now choose four other areas that need improvement.

The second step is you have to come up with reasons. It doesn't stop with the raising standards – that's where it starts – but finding empowering reasons for raising your standards is the key to change. Why do you want to raise your standards in those areas? What would it do for your current lifestyle, your current results, and what would it do for your future? I really want you to put some thought into why you should turn your "shoulds" into "musts," because as I've already explained, reasons come first, results come second. After you have the reasons, you'll have the strength and the motivation to follow through on raising your standards.

The third step in raising your standards is creating rituals. Rituals define us. All results in our lives start with the standards and then they're followed up with rituals. All successful people have rituals. They have routines and rituals for everything they do. They don't leave their success up to how they feel or luck or other people. They assure their success and they guarantee progress by creating results rituals and following through.

Success isn't about luck; it's about awareness. A ritual is something you do consistently that's been proven to get results. For example, if one of your standards is to lose weight, your reasons might be because you're sick of feeling this way, you want to feel healthier, you want to feel alive, you want people to be impressed by you, or you want to look better in your swimsuit. A ritual for successfully losing weight would be: to work out three times per week, to eat greens three days a week, to never eat past 7:30 p.m., to drink twice the amount of water you normally drink everyday, etc. All of these are rituals that, when done consistently, will help you reach your goal of losing weight. The more specific the goal, the more successful you'll be in achieving the goal.

The fourth step is finding role models. Find somebody who you can model who raises your standards and who's playing the game at a higher level than you. Study those who have standards that you're striving for. Read about them, listen to audios, watch videos, and immerse yourself in those who have already elevated their standards above society's standards. Society actually lowers people's standards. Don't base your standards on society's expectations or lack thereof. Eventually the standards you thought were too high are now the norm for you. That's the key. So find role models who elevate your circle of influence.

For some of you reading this, you might not necessarily know someone who's having a lot of success in their life. If that's you, go out and find audio books, follow someone on the Internet, get some mentoring through books, or even through courses. It doesn't necessarily have to be an individual one-on-one relationship at the beginning. That's actually how you develop more value and where you can reach out to higher-level people. I recently began reading *Think and Grow Rich* for the 17th time. Napoleon Hill passed away years ago, but he continues to inspire and teach through his books. You can find the same kind of mentorship in books too.

The fifth step is relentless discipline. Ultimately, discipline creates your lifestyle, and consistent discipline separates the extraordinary from the average. Self-discipline means doing the right thing whether you feel like it or not.

I remember Eric Thomas saying something that really stood out to me: "At the end of all your feelings is really nothing, but at the end of your principles and standards is a promise." If you do things based on your feelings, you're not going to get very far. Develop the relentless discipline to do what you need to do when you know you should do it, whether you feel like it or not. Start with little disciplines and keep building on those.

There's a quote that I used to read to my team all the time by Michael Jordan: "It's my standards that make me successful. Every day, I demand more from myself than anybody could humanly expect from me. I'm not competing against somebody else, I'm competing with what I'm capable of." You're competing with who you were yesterday, not your neighbor and not your friend. If you do these things consistently, you will be amazed by how much it elevates everything around you.

The speed of implementation is a huge part of success. What separates the mediocre from the extraordinary is how fast they implement. Implement what you learn. Don't be that person that says, "Oh, I'll do it later." Now matters more than ever. So take these steps and start raising your standards. Be better today than you were yesterday.

Chapter XII Action Steps:

1. Choose three areas of your life that you want to improve. Set high standards for each area.

2. List the reasons why you want to improve each area and what this change will mean for you, your lifestyle and your business.

3. Find role models either in person, audio, or in books that raise your standards and make you want to be better.

4. Practice relentless discipline. Set goals for each of these 3 areas and follow through. Make the action steps small at first and build upon the success.

5. Reward yourself when you succeed. This will encourage more discipline and you'll start seeing some incredible results.

XIII

Selling Yourself On You

Earlier, I brought up something very big for this chapter that will really help you make a big shift from using your feelings to focusing on what you should be doing instead. And really, this has to do with selling yourself. Not to other people, but selling yourself on you and regarding the tasks at hand. The reason why most people don't make progress is because they haven't actually sold themselves on the thing they are trying to do. Many people will start a business or a relationship or make a choice but they really haven't actually sold themselves on that business, person, or choice. To be clear – by "sold" I mean cut out *every* and *any* alternative. When you are sold on yourself, you know the importance of what you are doing, the purpose, and the ideal outcome you are striving for. If you are procrastinating or you're not getting things done, it's because you haven't actually sold yourself on that particular business, person or idea yet.

There are three ways to sell yourself on you and be more intentional with your actions:

The first way is to make sure what you're taking on is intentional and congruent with your goals of who you are. You want to take on more to become more, but you don't want to take on too much unless you are selling yourself on it. Instead of doing 20 things, do 3 things, but for each of those 3 things you need to sell yourself on them first. I usually pick 3 to 5 big ideas or activities that I know are helping my big vision and purpose and I focus on those. So, in order to sell yourself on you, don't take on too many different things at once. Instead, take on smaller, more focused steps and sell yourself on those so you're committed to doing them.

The second way is to have a series of questions or criteria for the things you do to make sure they have a purpose and an outcome that's worth your time. You need to have more reasons to do something and the reasons need to be logical and practical, and not just based on emotions. The reasons need to be more tangible so you will be able to finish and follow through at a higher level. This quote sums it up: "An immature mind jumps from task to task without finishing, but the mature mind stays on one task until completed." This applies to a relationship as well. If someone actually hasn't sold themselves on why the person they are with is the best person for them, then they'll still have that thought about somebody else out there being better for them, or worse, they won't be able to take the relationship they are in to the next level because they are not fully committed. So, if they don't sell themselves on the person, then they're not going to give their all in that relationship, and the same goes for business.

Here are some examples of questions or criteria that you might ask or use to assure you are sold. Is this congruent with my goals and vision for this campaign for this month? Is this going to require too much time for a very low return? Is this going to spread me too thin? Is this something I can scale at a higher level? Is this going to make me feel energized, enthusiastic and happy? Is this going to produce income? There are a lot of different questions you can ask, but the bottom line is making sure you are sold on it first. If you are sold, do it. In relation to your business, you'd want to ask:

"Is this something that's going to fit into the natural flow, or is this going to be an extra thing?" Any new project you take on should expand your current business, not be an extra little side thing that won't add value or bring revenue to your business. It should all be congruent, working together, and multiplying your efforts.

You have to always be thinking about why you're selling yourself. Example of selling yourself would be: "I'm waking up early because it's going to make me feel more energized." "I'm going to get bigger things done." "I'm going to gain more respect." "I'm going to get out of this money issue I have." "I'm going to become a better leader." "I'm going to be more fired up and excited." If you can sell yourself on waking up early, you're going to wake up early. Those who have quit smoking have sold themselves on why quitting is more important than smoking. It's all about selling yourself on what you want.

The third way to sell yourself is to stop doing things you aren't completely sold on and start having a greater focus on the things you are sold on. Don't get yourself involved in anything unless you're sold on the activity in front of you. In other words, if you don't know why you are doing it, stop doing it. The single biggest skill you can learn in business is to not get yourself involved if you haven't actually sold yourself on that activity yet. Time wise, effort wise, emotionally, don't get yourself involved unless you are sold.

Earlier, I mentioned criteria. What your main criteria should be depends on what stage you are at in life and business. If someone's broke and struggling and doesn't have money to pay rent, what should their criteria be? To make some freaking money! I met a guy at a coffee shop and he was complaining about how he was broke. I gave him about seven ideas on how to make money. But he kept making excuses against every single idea I had for him, so obviously he hasn't sold himself on why he should make money. He'll probably stay broke. You've got to figure out where you're at. For me, I make sure that what I take on is completely in tune with who I am, what I want, what my values are, and connects to my bigger picture.

The big key is you need to figure out what your criteria is ahead of time. You don't just want to make that list on the spot. Sit down and figure out what those criteria are beforehand. In my Game Changers Program, that's one of the things that we really dive deep into -- figuring out exactly the lifestyle you want, who you are, what you want, what your values are, and planning the best priorities and actions to take to reach your goals in the quickest way possible, to make sure you're intentional with all you do.

Chapter XIII Action Steps:

1. Figure out what stage you are at in business. Are you just starting out and need to make money? Is your business already established and making money but you want to go to the next level? Are you afraid to start a business and leave the safety of your full-time job?

2. What do you need to sell yourself on? Starting a business? Growing your business? Believing that you can earn the income you desire? Write it down.

3. For the next 30 days, every time you take an action, ask if that action gets you closer to what you want? If you consistently find that your actions don't move you closer, go back and list all the reasons you have for wanting what you want. Sell those reasons to yourself to build momentum.

XIV

Invest In Your Confidence Account

My next topic deals with something called, Your Confidence Account. I'm going to focus solely on how to elevate your confidence as an individual and reiterate why it's so important. Everybody has something inside called a confidence account. The size of that confidence account reflects how their current reality is forming, and it is in direct relation to what they *are* or *are not* achieving.

Can you name a visionary or an exceptional leader who lacked confidence? No, because there isn't one. They wouldn't have gotten to where they are without having confidence. So, where does confidence come from? Confidence comes from self-esteem, and that is a result of doing the things you know you should do when you know you should do them. Confidence in one's self and in one's abilities is crucial for achievement. It comes from doing what you need to do and following through, which builds self-esteem, and, ultimately, confidence. Your confidence level affects the reality of what you're accomplishing right now.

Why is a high confidence account so important to young entrepreneurs? It's important because you're going to take more risks, you're going to make more courageous decisions, and you're going to reach out to people who are playing the game at a higher level than you versus being fearful and remaining stuck. You're going to have to make important decisions. You're going to share your ideas even if they'll fail. Confidence is crucial today because the only job security people have right now is the confidence in their abilities and decisions. As your confidence increases, you feel more competent. You are better able to do the important tasks that need to be done. You're able to increase your skill level, and as your skills increase, your confidence account goes up.

All of this comes down to those seemingly little choices that affect your life and business, because the choices you made in the past have determined where you are right now. Having an unshakable confidence will cause you to stay levelheaded when nothing's going your way. Look at an exceptional athlete. He or she could miss 35 shots in a row, but guess what's going to come in the next play? Another shot. But take a player that's not confident: they miss a couple in a row, and they completely lose momentum. It's the same thing for entrepreneurs and business owners. There's nothing more powerful than self-confidence in multiplying your income by two, by three, by five, or by ten.

I used to tell my team you're either helping or hurting your confidence at all times. There's no in between. That means everything you do, every choice you make, every person you connect with, every social media post, every action you take, is either helping you get closer or further away from your goals. Most people don't think the little choices matter. But remember I talked about how, at age 65, only 2% of people are financially stable. When you gain clarity on your goals, on who you are, why you're doing what you're doing, your confidence increases.

People say I'm confident now, but there were times growing up where I felt inferior and I didn't want to reach out and be myself because I was scared of what others would think. I've been there and I know how that feels. But I also know the way to build up a confidence account and the tremendous rewards that come with confidence. What helps your confidence account? Increased income will help, recognition, awards, happy relationships, progress, personal growth audios, seminars, but the biggest way to boost your confidence account is sacrifice. When you stay in on a Friday night and you study and write down your goals instead of going out with friends, what do you think happens to your confidence account? When you wake up early and write your book (that you've been meaning to start) versus sleeping in, what do you think happens to your confidence account? When you reach out and you make those last couple of phone calls when you don't feel like it, your confidence goes up.

There are many ways to build your confidence account, but I have five tips that have worked well for me. The first tip is you have to ask, with every choice you make, "Will this choice help or hurt my confidence?" Successful people make choices based on who they want to become versus feeling comfortable in the moment. One of the people who made a big impact on me early in my career was Isaac Tolpin, and his entire company now is focused on the term "Choose Growth." You always have two choices, the hard one and the easy one. When you choose growth in the moment, your confidence increases. I want you to start making decisions right now based on your standards and goals versus your emotions and feelings.

The second tip is your perspective on challenges helps your confidence or kills it. If you feel like challenges are bad and you should never have challenges and you try to avoid them, your confidence is going to go down, because any time you set goals, there will be challenges. But having the perspective that challenges help build your character, make you more intelligent, expand your outlook, builds your confidence because you embrace growth, even during challenging times. A challenge should strengthen you because you're gaining experience. Understanding challenges is a good thing, and definitely boosts your confidence. There's a quote from Eminem that drives this point home: "The moment I used my adversity to my advantage, my career exploded." I don't care if you like Eminem or not, you have to respect someone who came from nothing and is now worth over $150 million. Using adversity and challenges to your advantage builds character and increases your confidence.

The third tip is, when you stay consistent and you start seeing results, your confidence rises. And this correlates with the fourth tip, which is get out of your comfort zone regularly. Are you doing things that scare you? Are you getting uncomfortable on a daily basis? Focus on doing things that are uncomfortable in the moment because that builds your courage. The fifth tip is never compare yourself to others. This is a big one and will kill your confidence quicker than anything else. Don't let other people's opinions guide your choices. Tune out all the people who are negative. When you're an entrepreneur, you get a lot of negativity/doubt. The only person you should compare yourself to is the person you were yesterday. If you start comparing yourself to your own progress each day, you're going to build a high level of confidence.

Chapter XIV Action Steps:

1. Take note of your confidence account. Are you hurting or helping your confidence account?

2. Use one of these five tips and start practicing building your confidence account.

3. Make a commitment to yourself today to stop comparing yourself to others. Focus solely on your own progress and improving your business and life.

XV

How To Build Mental Toughness

This next topic is extremely important for all entrepreneurs: mental toughness. I want to talk about what mental toughness really is, how to develop it, and the benefits of mental toughness for your business, future, peace of mind and happiness. I'll discuss overall mental toughness, what it is, and give you some steps on how to develop this asset in your life.

First, what is mental toughness? What do you do when nothing goes your way? What do you do when everything that you've planned fails, when your business is failing, or there's an emergency or a death in the family? What do you do when you're squeezed? What do you do in critical situations?

Dan Kennedy taught me that high tolerance for pressure is a skill successful entrepreneurs need, and it is something they are paid great dividends for. Do you fold under pressure or do you look for solutions? Do you dwell on mistakes or do you use them to improve your performance? Mental toughness means having the ability to stay calm and focused during turmoil, failure and chaos. As the economy tightens, it's especially important to hone this skill. It can be revolutionary for your future, your career, family, income, and the influence you have on others.

Mental toughness is developed over a period of time. It takes years, not days or weeks. It's about pushing yourself and it's built through really tough times. It separates the men from the boys, the women from the girls, the successful from the average. People who exercise this mental muscle and persevere ultimately succeed at a higher level than everybody else. As you know and may have experienced, most people give up before they succeed. All you need to remember to succeed is to keep going, keep showing up, and keep pushing forward.

Here's an example, imagine you are in front of a fire hydrant and suddenly water starts to gush out. You're sitting in front of it and it keeps gushing out harder and harder. You will either get pushed to the side, or you will keep taking it. And say something like, "Is that all you got water? Bring it!"

Think of mental toughness as being able to take on more and more without losing yourself in what's happening. During times like these, when you're being pushed and challenged, is when you build your capacity and your strength, and ultimately, your mental toughness. You either become a mentally tough person, or you give up. The more you take on, the bigger you want to become, the more water that's coming out of the fire hydrant. If you can't handle it, you get pushed to the side, and you won't develop mental toughness. If you keep going and you keep pushing, eventually, you'll build your tolerance for handling challenges and your mental toughness will rise.

Now, you might be wondering, how can I develop my mental toughness? One way is to just take on more to become more. Instead of saying, "I'm going to go to school *or* I'm going to work," go to school *and* work. Instead of thinking, "I'm going to start this business *or* I'm going to keep my job," start the business *and* keep your job. Challenge yourself. The first thing is take on more to become more. Try to take on more and expand your capacity every chance you get. When I think about how busy I am or how much I am taking on, I think of Steve Jobs. He was running Pixar and Apple at the same time at one point. If someone's complaining about being busy, I say, "Steve Jobs ran two billion dollar companies at the same time. Are you really expanding your capacity?" That's the kind of thinking and doing that builds mental toughness.

An investment in persistence is a big perspective flipper. Understand that mental toughness is really an investment in your future success. There isn't a book or seminar that can help you develop this mental strength. Only by working through challenges, hanging in when it gets tough, and being fully committed to seeing your goals through will build mental toughness. It's like buying a bond or watching grass grow. It happens slowly. So take on more to become more, and realize this is an investment in persistence.

There's a big difference between responding versus reacting. Your reaction influences people more than you realize, and especially your confidence. So don't react, just respond with intelligence. All great leaders stay even emotionally, and you really can't tell if a successful person's having a good or bad day. Now, if someone's not mature enough, and they don't have mental toughness, when something doesn't go their way, what do they usually do? They get upset, they get flustered, or they get angry, and you're able to tell that something's wrong. You know someone's not mentally tough if they show a lot of emotion when things don't go their way. I'm not saying emotion is bad, but one of my mentors told me that when you're in a leadership role you don't want to show you're tired, you're hungry, or you're frustrated because people will lose respect for you subconsciously. People want strong leaders and strong entrepreneurs around them. So how quickly do you adapt and adjust to challenges? Do you show your emotions when things get hard or do you take a bit of time to determine the best course of action? Respond, don't react.

People are so caught up in personal growth. I always say learning is easy. Implementation is hard. That's why so many people learn, but so few implement. You can't get mentally tough by learning all day long. How do you become mentally tough? By doing, applying, and implementing what you learn to reach your goals. The second you set bigger goals and take on more, challenges will arise, and you'll be tested to see if you deserve that success. Welcome challenges. Most people lower their standards when they get disappointed, and that's a guaranteed way to fail. When you're disappointed, get more disciplined. That only comes with persistence.

Good thoughts and actions can never produce bad results, but bad thoughts and actions can never produce good results. If you don't discipline your disappointment, you're going to have a rough ride as an entrepreneur. I try to turn my disappointment into drive and curiosity. That way, I understand that I'm building my mental toughness, I'm taking the right approach, I'm responding versus reacting, and I'm eventually going to reach a higher level. Lean into those challenges and get excited when challenges come your way because it's a new opportunity for you to expand your mental toughness, a new opportunity for you to build new skills, and reach a new level in your life and your business. If you're not failing, you've got to start, because the more you fail, the more successful you'll become.

You can also study people who you feel are mentally tough and persistent. Model that behavior and you'll build your mental strength. If you can respond versus react and welcome challenges, you'll start to see great results. Remember, with every choice you make you're either becoming mentally tougher or mentally weaker, and it's those decisive moments that really make all the difference.

Chapter XV Action Steps:

1. The next time you have a challenge or are faced with an important decision, welcome this opportunity with excitement.

2. Take time to think about possible solutions to this challenge or problem before taking any action.

3. Respond, don't react. No matter how disappointed, frustrated or angry you feel, take a few deep breaths and remove yourself until you are in a calmer, more focused state. Focus your attention on the problem, not the person. Analyze.

XVI

Six Personal Insights To 10x Your Life

A lot of people these days are using spirituality as an excuse for not producing. Don't get me wrong. If you're going to get into spirituality and the Law of Attraction, and similar concepts, that's amazing. I fully support that. But don't use it without actually focusing on results as well. Being spiritual without focusing on results will leave you broke. If you're going to be spiritual, make sure you have an emphasis on actually producing something. And this leads me to some of the biggest lessons I've learned about business and success.

One of my biggest lessons is the importance of having a team. I've had big teams. I've had small teams. There have also been times when I only had me. What I know for sure is you can't do it by yourself. You need a solid team around you so you can purely focus on your strengths and what you're good at. I've tried to do too many things at once. I have a great team, but I've tried to do certain things I don't enjoy or I'm not good at myself because I'm a hands-on guy. And it's just not effective. It gives me a headache and stresses me out and it leaves my team feeling unappreciated and undervalued. You can't do the entrepreneur thing by yourself. You need someone to do your marketing. You need someone to manage all the accounting. You need a team to promote your products and services. You need an editor. You need an executive assistant as you grow your business. You need someone who does websites, design, visuals, pictures, and knows what produces results. You need a team builder to build your company. Find or build a dream team around you and figure what you need and who you need to reach your company goals.

The second lesson I've learned is you need to spend money to make money. In my last business, I was spending a lot of money per month on recruiting, marketing, advertising, prizes, and visuals, but I wasn't putting money back into the business. I heard four top CEO's say the two things they spend money on are themselves and their business. And when I say on themselves, I don't mean they spend money on things they can consume, but they invest in their ideas and put money towards mastermind groups, seminars, programs, or anything else that helps them grow and develop.

When I was hired to motivate a sales team in Las Vegas for one of the largest talent agencies in the world, the owner told me every single thing he makes goes back in his company. You're not going to become wealthy by stockpiling all of your business earnings. You're going to become wealthy by investing, whether it's in yourself, in a mastermind program, in your business, or in a community like Game Changers. That's how you become wealthy. Before I learned this important lesson, I was trying to make sure everything was running at a high level, making good money, and inspiring people, but not spending anything. And it just doesn't work. You have to spend money to make money. Spend money on things that will help your business grow forward, or things that will help elevate your standards, your game, your mindset, your marketing, your product, or your team.

The third lesson I learned is the importance of focusing on the task at hand until it's complete. Not until I feel like stopping, but until it's completed. A lot of people will work on something, and they think, "Time's up. I'm done." Why not do it right the first time, and why not work on it until you're finished? *Most people stop when they feel like it. Champions stop when they're finished.* That's a great quote, which I have taken to heart. I have created a great system that works for me and maybe it can work for you. When I'm working on something, I do so in 60 to 90 minute increments, take a short break, and then go back a do another 60-90 minute block. I continue to do this until it's done right and completely. If you do something right the first time, you don't have to do it again. And it's important to notice that I set myself a time. If I go a little over, that's fine, but during that time I'm working hard and not letting myself get distracted from the task at hand.

The forth lesson I learned is to value excellence over quantity. You've got to realize, when you're doing something online, it's your legacy. Your kids, grandkids and great grandkids are going to see it. I'm a high results guy. I always want to go, go, go. So sometimes I need to take a deep breath, try not to do too much at once, and focus on service and excellence instead of pumping out a ton of stuff. Make sure you're showing up every day charged and having a lot of fun. I'm showing up every day charged and extremely motivated because I'm remembering my goals while I'm doing what I need to. So keep that in mind. Always show up charged and have fun while building your business.

The fifth lesson is to focus on longer-term relationships. Here's what I want you to do. I want you to add value to people with zero expectations back. Most people go to events, and they're mentality is, "What can I get?" But what's going to give you the best value and the best return on your investment is if you give. Give everybody everything that you know. It'll come back to you in multiple ways.

A lot of people want my time, and it's the people that not only give, but also live their best life. They help me without even expecting anything. For instance, there's a guy who has recommended twelve people to my program, and they've all been rock stars. He believes in our community so much because he's seen such a difference in his own results, in his network, in his mindset, in his flexibility, and in his freedom. It's unreal. He doesn't ask me, "Could I have your time?", but anytime he needs it, I help him. I'll take an hour out of my day to help him. I'll send him leads for his company. I'll do all kinds of stuff for him because he was so willing to give.

It's the people who just want to take, take, take that I don't really respect. So if you want to get a hold of someone successful, go promote their stuff first. Share their articles. Ask them what you can do for them. And don't say right after, "Okay, I need something now from you now." Focus on longer-term relationships, add as much value as possible, and quit expecting things in return. If you do this, it'll come back to you twentyfold, I promise.

I have one final lesson in this chapter. In everything you do, think huge and act bigger, because that's the best way to stay motivated and focused. People say, "What if you don't hit your goals?" So what? You're at least thinking big, and your results are going to be much better than if you didn't think big at all or you aimed low. The problem is not that people are aiming too high and missing. The problem is that they aim too low and they hit. You need to start writing down your goals every day. Write down goals that are scary to you. Goals like I'm going to make my first six figures in the next six months, I'm going to buy two houses next year, or I'm going to write two books. You won't believe how motivated you get when you write down your goals. So I challenge you to do that right now. Right now! Review them. Reread the lessons I've learned, and think about what you've learned in the last six months and take those lessons and experiences and invest in them over the next six months of your journey. You'll experience some pretty astounding breakthroughs.

XVII

Using the Decision Train to Take Action

Get out a piece of paper or your laptop. I'm going to talk about something called the decision train, and I promise, when I talk about this, you're going to want to remember it. If you're 23 years old now, you won't forget it even when you're 50. It's made a drastic difference in my early success.

The reason I can make that promise is because I know a lot of people have said that this has radically helped their mindset and their physical results, so I know it works. Most people are broke, and most people are stressed, unhappy, unhealthy, regretful, frustrated, are in bad relationships, confused and unclear and they've given up on their dreams. One in three Americans believes their best chance of becoming wealthy is by winning the lottery. Are you kidding me?

There are three trains. The first train is a feelings train. Most people in society make every single decision based on their feelings. If they don't feel like working out, guess what? They don't work out. If they don't feel like waking up early, guess what? They sleep in late. If they don't feel like getting their book done or doing their homework, or if they don't feel like doing what they're supposed to, they don't do it. The next train is the actions train. From their feelings, they take a specific action – or no action – and usually it's no action. The third train is the decision train.

They decide to not do anything. So when they feel like not working out, they don't take any action, and what's their decision? "I'm not going to work out." And that's how they live their lives, based on their feelings.

At the end of every value, principle, and discipline is a promise. Here's what the 5% do. There are people right now who are energized, they have clarity, they're having fun, they have financial freedom, they have a great lifestyle, they're confident, and have amazing relationships. Do you want to know why? They flip these trains and go in a different direction. Unsuccessful people take this track: feelings, actions, decisions, and that's how they end up broke, stressed and struggling. Successful people make decisions first. When they decide something, that's what they do, period, regardless of how they feel. Then from that decision, they take action, and how do you think they feel afterwards? They're excited, they're energized, and they're more confident because they've made that decision. They followed through and they got results.

One of the biggest ways to build your self-esteem is to do what you say you're going to do. Every time you say you're going to do something and don't do it, your confidence level goes down. What successful people do is they decide, "I'm going to work out five times this week." And they follow through.

The biggest key to success and productivity is making decisions not in the moment, but beforehand. Successful people decide what they're going to do, they take action regardless of how they feel, and, as an end result, they feel exceptional. Their confidence increases, their self-respect increases, and their income increases. It's an upward spiral from there. If you want to be like the top entrepreneurs in the country, you need to decide ahead of time what you're going to get done, and commit. Once you've done that, take action regardless of how you feel in the current moment, and you won't believe the type of energy and success you'll see right away because you're making the harder decision. That's really what the decision train is, and I know how powerful it is because I've done it for years, and it's made a huge difference for me and for the people I've coached.

Sometimes I don't feel like doing something, but I've already decided to do it because I know it's part of my mission and it helps people. I might be tired, I might have other things to do, but if I already made the decision, I commit. And every single time, when I'm finished, I feel exceptional. But it's hard. If it were easy everyone would be successful.

Here's how to drive your decision train in the right direction. Be aware of how you are doing things now. Second, make sure your goals are written down and you revisit them once or twice a week. Think through your week with intelligence based on your priorities. Make sure you're getting things done based on your priorities versus how you feel. The key is looking at your goals consistently. When you don't feel like doing something, remind yourself that when you actually made that decision, or when you made your

schedule, you were in an intelligent mindset and you were in a success mindset. When you made that decision, you were thinking about your future self and success. Think back when you made that schedule and stick with that decision. Look at your goals daily. Create some type of ritual that motivates you when you don't feel like doing something. Maybe put your favorite song on or do something that gets you back in the zone. Do whatever you need to to keep your decision train moving in the right direction. Remember, decisions first, actions second, and feelings are a result of following through on
your decision.

XVIII

The Power Of Asking Questions

Now let's talk about the power of questions, and how important it is to ask the right questions to benefit your future. Asking questions is an excellent way to give you clarity about where you are, why you are where you are, and it helps you design a more compelling future. I asked the right questions that have made me an extra 40 to 50 grand in one year. What questions should you be asking?

Two of the most powerful questions are: "Are you really living your calling or your mission? Are you living in a way that you know is maximizing your strengths and bringing out your creative genius?" These are such important questions, because if you're not, they help you figure out why not. Here's two more powerful questions: "Are you enjoying what you're doing, and does it play to your strengths? If not, why are you doing it?" For instance, let's say you're in college, but you don't like it and you don't know why you're even going, and you have no job attached to what you are learning. Why are you in college if you don't feel like it's making you sing and you're not super pumped about it? Now, college is great if you know exactly why you're there and you have a job lined up, if you're becoming a lawyer, or a doctor, or a sports agent. But if you're just doing it because other people do it, that is a terrible reason.

Are you really giving your best daily? I ask myself this question all the time. Am I really giving my best daily? If not, why am I not giving my best daily? Why am I selling myself short?

How often are you looking at your yearly goals? What time are you waking up? What's important about your morning routine? What questions spark your mind? What are you doing to challenge yourself? If you aren't challenging yourself daily, you're not going to make real progress. I would spend some time answering these kinds of questions because the questions you ask yourself consistently determine how your life turns out and determine your current reality.

Questions can really influence the way you think. By asking good questions, you're able to get better answers that lead you in the right direction. You need to be asking yourself some of those deeper thinking questions, but also the questions that are almost like check-in questions. An example of a check-in question is, "Is this helping me achieve my goals?" This question keeps me on track and I have it on a post it note on my computer.

You need to have questions for help, questions for progress, questions for your character and for family. One of my biggest questions, when I was a young manager and my goal was to do $1 million in sales for the year, was, "Am I thinking and acting like a million dollar manager?" The year before, when I only made $750,000, can you guess how I was thinking and acting? Like a $750,000 manager, so that's what I got. A lot of people are thinking and acting like a broke college student, but they want to be a successful millionaire. It doesn't work that way. You've got to think and act like a successful person.

Are you truly moving forward, or are you falling behind? Are you truly progressing towards your goals, or are you falling behind? How do you feel when you read that? Think about it. There's no in-between. You're either moving forward or going backwards. Are you truly moving towards your dreams, or are you simply conning yourself into believing that that there is a right time and you're just waiting for it, like broke people do?

Are you doing things that you enjoy, or not? I like to delegate everything I don't enjoy. I work too hard to do things I don't like. If I had to put all of my podcast stuff together, and do all the things that go into making a podcast, I would sit in a room and I would hit my head against the side of the door. That's too much for one person to do, and there are people who have already mastered the pieces I don't enjoy doing. Are you truly being yourself or are you adapting to society's standards? Are you really being authentic in every situation? I'm always authentic, and I've grown to be who I am, which is not always the person people want me to be. I don't want to adapt so people like me. I want to be me, and the right people will gravitate towards me.

Are your relationships truly supporting you at the highest level, or not? This is another powerful one. Do you truly believe in yourself, or are you still focused on limitations? Do you really believe you can be the top in the country at whatever it is that you want to do? Do you really believe you can make your first million dollars? Do you really believe you can be the number one network marketer in your company? Do you really believe that you can make a million by the time you're 18, like Houston Gunn did? If not, what do you have to do to get yourself to a Level 10 belief that you can hit that goal? Constantly ask these kinds of questions to gain clarity about what you believe is possible for you.

Are you really fit and healthy, or aren't you? "Sometimes, someday, tomorrow" are words used by people who will always struggle. Remove those words from your vocabulary. Are you truly building wealth, or are you depleting it? Are you building sustainable income and wealth, or are you spending more than you're making? Are you truly stepping up, or are you backing down? We're not taught in school how to ask critical thinking questions. What's taught in school is memorizing the past like what happened in Germany in 1973 or what happened to the Appalachian Mountains or about what Christopher Columbus did. When you start asking the right questions, the tough questions, and take the time to answer them truthfully, you'll begin to understand what is holding you back from succeeding and what you need to do to move forward.

Chapter XVIII Action Steps:

1. Pick out a couple questions that mean the most to you and answer them honestly.

2. Once you have your answers, try and do something different in that area. For instance, if your relationships suck, work on communication. If you are not reaching your business goals because you don't feel like you deserve success, start focusing on why you do deserve success.

3. Repeat this exercise using a different question once you have gained clarity on the first one.

XIX

Six Steps To Change In 90 Days

Right now, I'm going to give you the 3-90-1 rule that I use called the "Game Changers Envision Exercise." This exercise really helped me grow my sales team, my income, and brought my office sales close to $8 million.

There are so many different outlets in personal growth, tactics, books, and audios and that's great, but you need to narrow down your focus and simplify. Pick three main goals you want to accomplish in the next 90 days. Most people do yearly goals, 3-year goals, 5-year goals; it's tough to do that because you lose motivation, and what happens is people wait until the end of the year to focus on their yearly goals. Focusing on three main goals for 90-day increments is very effective and sustainable.

Next, figure out the one skill that you need to master in order to make sure you hit those three goals. All your personal growth, all your audios, all your podcasts, everything you do is focused around that one skill or one tactic that is congruent with those three goals. The envision exercise has helped me reach my biggest goals and I know, if you apply this, it can help you reach yours.

Envision your business 90 days from now. Get really detailed in your vision. How many people are on your team? How much money are you making? How much do you want to have saved in your account? What's the culture of your team? How are you feeling? What systems are in place? Then fast-forward and work backwards. Determine exactly how you want your life to be 90 days from now.

What qualities have you attained accomplishing those three goals? Fast-forward 90 days again. What I used to do is think is, "Okay, in 90 days my business will be here, I'll have this motivated team, and we'll be making over $2 million in revenue. Here are the qualities I've attained: I'm a stronger leader, I have more integrity, I have better character, I'm a lot more positive, I'm more disciplined, I'm a better listener, I'm persistent, and I have a better work ethic." The key here though is to use this exercise to understand the qualities you're lacking right now that are needed to get the results you want.

When I was brand new to business, I saw a lot of ways to cut corners and make easy money. One thing I worked on was having the utmost integrity. I noticed that successful people had integrity. When you work on something, you become better at it. I also worked on my attitude. Sometimes I would make problems bigger than they were and I'd get in a negative state. So, I started working on these weaknesses and I became a better listener, had a stronger work ethic and was more disciplined. It didn't happen overnight. But by becoming aware of what I was lacking, I was able to improve upon those qualities that were holding me back.

What qualities do you lack right now that you need in order to get to those 3 goals in 90 days? If you really want to accomplish those goals, then it will take a lot more than hope and ambition. It actually takes figuring out what you need to work on so you can figure out the person you need to be to hit those goals. You need to look at that list and ask yourself which of these qualities you lack the most. When you put down your qualities of what you've attained in 90 days, then you look at it and say "What do I need to work on the most right now?" Identify the gap in those qualities, and then figure out which one you want to work on first. Pick that, work on it, and track your progress.

One of my weakest areas was planning my day. I haphazardly went about my days instead of making a plan. Over time, I learned to plan my day according to my priorities and, eventually, I became a master at this. Successful people know what they want and what they need to consistently work on to reach their goals. Be like other successful people and determine what you want, get clearer on those three goals, and then figure out what qualities you need to attain those goals. Include how you want to feel at the end of your 90 days. Do you want to feel proud? Excited? More motivated? Accomplished? Knowing how you want to feel and working towards that feeling is a great motivator for keeping you on track.

Finally, you need a personal growth plan and you need coaches. You need to learn from everything you do. I kept a journal and I documented everything I learned and I kept reaching out to people who were already achieving what I wanted. I chose my books carefully, I chose who I was around carefully, and everything I did was an investment in being more effective in order to reach those three goals. I became a lot more intentional, and looking back, I did reach those goals.

I have a phenomenal program that works for many entrepreneurs in helping them grow and take their life to the next level, called the Game Changers Academy. It is invite only because we're very selective about whom we accept, but I've created a two week gold level trial so more people can be successful. They can try it out and get a taste of it, and what's cool is they can get some exceptional wisdom, some amazing strategies, cutting-edge techniques, and world class training right away. If it's not for them, they can choose to leave, but if it is for them, then we'll see if they qualify for the platinum version. It's a fantastic opportunity for people to break free of their limits, install some amazing habits, and be around some of the most success-oriented people on the planet. It can really help you learn how to be an elite performer and how to take your business to a level you didn't even think was possible. We also have many guest speakers like Brian Tracy, Grant Cardone, and other well-known success leaders.

If you are interested in trying it out, you can learn more at **GameChangersMovement.com**.

Chapter XIX Action Steps:

1. Try the 3-90-1 plan now. Use the envision exercise to see where you want to go, what you want to achieve and how you want to feel 90 days from today.

XX

Stay Charged With These Five Keys

Anyone who knows me knows I'm very energetic and hyper. In this chapter, I'll share the keys to having more energy and how to stay charged while you are building or starting your business.

Energy is such an important resource, especially for an entrepreneur because we have lots of things to do. It can be a crazy busy life so it's important to tackle it all, but to do that, you need high energy. The last six years, I've studied how to create energy on demand because it's so important for my business and my personal life.

Even if you have all of the time and money in the world, it won't matter if you don't have energy. If you don't feel alive and vibrant you're not going to want to do anything or get anything done. It's important that you stay focused on what matters, how you feel and the energy you have inside. You need a zest for life, to be pumped to take on the day, take on the week, and take on the month. Here are a couple of strategies that have helped me stay energized, charged, and focused at all times.

Clarity. When you have clarity and know what you're doing for at least 90 days, you have clear direction, and that will automatically keep you more energized. When you're busy and when you're frustrated and unclear, it's so easy to get demotivated or discouraged. When you're discouraged or when you're overwhelmed, you seek out distractions. Those feelings are uncomfortable so we tend to run from them by finding a distraction. That's how your brain works.

What you have to ask yourself is: "Do my daily activities match my vision for the future?" "Do I have an intention in my daily activities?" These are two of the most important questions you can ask because with clarity comes energy and confidence. So get crystal clear on the activities that yield the highest results, and then make sure you prioritize those in your schedule. These priorities should be activities that are strictly for you, not somebody else. They are ones that even if nothing else gets done, if you do these, you will still feel a sense of accomplishment.

The second key is that you have to take control of your activities and your agenda, so you can literally speak your future into existence. By doing so, you are predetermining what you're doing, instead of letting outside circumstances control your outcomes. Once you get clear, make sure you have your priorities and then refuse interference. When you are focused and intentional you have a lot more excitement and clarity.

A third key is to focus on gratitude and realize that you can always be grateful for something. Every time I am stressed or not energized I think about what I'm grateful for, and then I shift my focus to what I want as well. This is huge as far as productivity and staying charged goes.

The fourth key is you have to make sure you watch what you put in your body because usually what you put in your body affects how you feel and what you look like. In the same way, what you put in your mind is how you think and what you do. Most people put bad things in their mind: news, gossip, magazines, and their action level is very low and their attitude very bad. They put bad food in their body so they do not look healthy.

How do you think their energy is if they put bad food in their body? It is going to be minimal at best. Consider this: do you feel the difference in your energy level when you eat good food or when you eat bad food? When you eat the right food and consume smaller portions, your energy level increases. There are two ways to increase physical energy and stay charged: nutrition and exercise. Nutrition is a huge part of your daily energy and appropriate nutrition means managing what you put in your body, how much you eat, and realizing what foods bring you energy and what foods take it away. Try to add at least one healthy food to your diet each day and drink lots of water. You'll notice a difference and that will motivate you to eat healthier naturally.

Here are some tips that really helped me increase my energy and improve my overall health:

1. Avoid anything processed, that you can't pronounce, and of course fast food. It is really bad for your energy. Stick with organic and fresh foods. I focus on the energy the food gives me. Once you start eating fresher foods, you'll start craving them.

2. Do your best to ALWAYS have greens in your meals. Whether it's cucumbers, mixed green salad, broccoli, spinach, celery, wheatgrass, green beans, kale, etc., make sure to add something fresh and alive from the ground versus processed or repurposed foods. Avoid foods that have been manufactured in any way. Something my fiancé Kayla always says is to ask yourself this question before eating: "Will this clog me or cleanse me?" (I think she got it from Tony Robbins though - ha!)

3. Drink water 30 minutes before and 30 minutes after each meal. That was a game changer for me. It helps the food go down smoother, aids in digestion and clears out your system. Having extra water helps flush out anything that is sticking and causing your body to work harder. When your body has to work harder, you lose precious energy.

4. Eat smaller portions. I eat until I have enough, not until I'm extremely full. The portions in America have been proven to be much larger than anywhere else in the world -- that explains a lot, huh? You do not want to eat to the point to where you feel bloated or too full to do anything. Not only do you gain a lot of weight, bad weight, but this makes you tired and lethargic. The digestive process is one of the body's most energy-consuming processes. When you eat more than necessary, it will take more energy away from you.

5. Don't eat past 7-7:30 p.m. If you eat at 10:00 p.m., you won't sleep as well and you'll wake up tired because your body is working so hard to digest that food instead of resting like it should.

All of these tips will help you feel better and increase your energy. And it's not difficult to find good foods to eat. You want foods that are high alkaline and organic. Go on a seven-day challenge where you avoid all processed food. Don't eat any fast food, don't eat past 7:30 p.m., eat smaller portions, and drink tons of water.

I did a 10-day challenge a year ago and I went alkaline and didn't eat any meat. It was pretty much a vegan diet. I felt more energy than I'd ever had in my life. I would wake up at 5:00 a.m. energized like I never had felt before. Then at 3:00 or 4:00 in the afternoon I was still energized, which is incredible. The energy doubles when you exercise consistently five or six days a week. Exercise can bring you a lot of energy because you can feel the effects of exercise 10 or 12 hours afterwards. If you can add that piece, I highly recommend getting exercise at least three times per week.

Focusing on the priorities, getting clear on what you want, and then making sure you put the right foods into your body are key. It's important that you make sure you're doing everything you can to give yourself an advantage for increasing your energy.

The fifth and biggest key is being extremely passionate about what you do. It's really about having a mission and realizing that what you're doing is bigger than you. When you are part of a mission or a movement, basically when you're doing something that's impacting more people and you know this is your calling, there's nothing else that can motivate you more or increase your energy level. People like Gary Vaynerchuk and Eric Thomas admit they do not always work out. They're not always the healthiest, but they have more energy than some 22-year-olds I know. Eric is 41 and Gary is 37, but they have more energy than people half their age. It's because they're so dialed in and focused on what they want that nothing can stop them. Even if they're tired, what they do and who they're becoming and the impact they're making causes them to be fired up and excited to keep pushing forward.

What I always try to do is look for everything that can give me an advantage. I'm not talking about only getting an advantage over my competition or other people that do the same thing as me, but anything to get me closer to the goals and dreams that I've set for myself. Use your passion as your number one motivator. And then follow the keys in this chapter to gain sustainable energy to see you through.

XXI

How To Create Consistent Energy In Your Life

This chapter is all about consistent energy and motivation, and why this is so important for young entrepreneurs. The reality of life is energy. You're nothing without energy. You could have all the success, you could have all the money and all the flexibility, but if you don't have energy, you won't be able to sustain. You're not going to be at your productive best, you're not going to produce, you're not going to add value, you're not going to connect with people well, and you're not going to be there for your family. Energy is crucial to achievement in this new economy.

So how do you actually go about maintaining that energy? Many entrepreneurs out there are really full of energy, on a high, and they're on the peak of that rollercoaster. But then, at other times, they just seem to be dragging their feet and can barely get out of bed. So the question is how do you actually maintain a high level of consistent energy? The major problem is people don't have the energy to really go after their biggest dreams and goals. They're tired during the day, they don't want to wake up, and they're lethargic.

Stress, worry, and not having clarity cause a massive drain on your energy. When you have a lot of stuff in your head, a lot of stuff to do or you have things that you haven't finished yet, your energy is depleted. People don't think about energy that way, but when you're stressed out, your energy goes way down. So, let's start with clearing your mind. Write everything down and prioritize what's important to you so you can get it out of your head. One option is every week, do what I call a 50-minute focus finder. Set a timer, sit down with a couple sheets of paper, and for 50 minutes write down everything, every project, everything that comes to your mind. When you clear your mind and get everything out of your head, you'll feel a sense of relief. Then once you write everything down, you can start to prioritize what matters using these four tips. First, cross out what you can't change or you can't control. It's a waste of worry and as Brian Tracy says, "The two worst things in life are excuses and worrying." So if you can't control it, get it out of your head and don't worry about it. Next, figure out what you can delegate to somebody else. Third, determine what has to get done by a certain date and put it in your schedule. Finally, determine what items need action right now. After you have everything organized and you put it into your schedule, your mind will be focused on what matters and you'll be able to start building momentum.

The second is to eat healthier, period. What you put in your body determines how you feel just as what you put in your mind determines what you do. Instead of eating two or three big meals a day, eat four to five times a day but smaller portions. This will increase your metabolism and your energy level. Drink lots of water. Carry a large bottle of water with you at all times and refill it throughout the day.

Besides clearing your mind and eating healthy, it's important to have a powerful morning routine. How you start your day is one of the most important factors in determining your energy and success, and ultimately it affects what you get done each day. The whole point of a morning routine is to give you courage, energy and confidence to start your day, so you go out in the world charged and excited. A morning routine sets your intention, which means you actually know exactly what you're going to get done. Stop hitting the snooze button. When you do that you're literally resisting life, and you don't want to be one of those people who hits the snooze button. Make a decision the night before about what time you will wake up and decide to be excited, juiced, motivated, and inspired each new day. Here's my morning routine: I decide the night before when I'm going to wake up. If you go to sleep thinking about your goals and being excited, you'll wake up inspired. The first thing I do when I wake up is drink a huge bottle of water and I energize my body, because you can't separate your body from your mind. When you become stronger physically, you're stronger mentally. Then I do a 20 to 25-minute workout six days a week. Then I read something positive that sparks my mind, makes me think or challenges me for 25 to 30 minutes. Next, I review my day and make sure my priorities are straight. When you review your day and you know your priorities, you get more energized and you attack the day with focus and intention. The last thing I do is I visualize. I visualize and I look at my goals for the year and for the next couple years and I just imagine what it feels like to hit those goals. When you get up and do inner work, when you get up early and focus on yourself, it does wonders because the most important person in your life is you. And when you do that and you go to bed on time and you wake up early, it not only gives you confidence, but also increases energy.

Start exercising every morning. I already talked about morning routines, but it's so important for consistent energy. When I'm getting tired, I'll work out at 5:00 p.m. I'll do a quick cardio or I'll run for ten minutes just to refocus my mind. Because when you're building big business and when you really have goals to be the best entrepreneur you can be or create an amazing lifestyle, you're not working the 9:00 to 5:00 like most people. They say 9:00 to 5:00 is when you make your living, after hours is when you create your legacy. Schedule your workouts now for the rest of this month in your calendar. Make them nonnegotiable, unmovable and the most important part of your week. The most important appointment you can keep is the one you make with yourself. Focus on how good you're going to feel after each workout and the energy you're going to have. Muhammad Ali said, "I didn't like any of my early morning runs but I liked the idea of being a world champion." You don't have to like the idea of waking up early, but you should like the idea of living a world-class life and being a world-class entrepreneur.

Chapter XXI Action Steps:

1. Choose one tip from this chapter to increase your energy. Make a commitment to yourself and mark it in your calendar.

2. Don't miss your appointment with yourself. Follow through consistently for 30 days. After that, your new energy exercise will become a habit.

3. Use another tip from this chapter and repeat steps 1 and 2. Continue doing this until you are satisfied with your level of
consistent energy.

XXII

Why You Need A Morning Routine

One question I get asked a lot is about the importance of morning routines. I've been asked this even more frequently this year as people are beginning to understand the importance of having one. A morning routine is critical for many reasons.

First, it's like an athlete going into the game. If someone just goes straight into the game without any visualization or practice or warm-up, they aren't going to play well. It's the same for everyday life, entrepreneurship, and business. A morning routine gets you into the right mindset and makes you more disciplined. It also sets the tone and helps you make better choices throughout the day. I've noticed personally how productive I am when I do my morning routine and how lethargic and nonproductive I am when I don't. All successful people have a great morning routine that's congruent with their goals.

What actually makes up a good morning routine? What should you incorporate in your life? All of these are important questions. Your morning routine depends on when you wake up. Some people wake up a lot earlier than others, but you have to get it out of your head that you're not a morning person. That's just a limiting belief. The first thing I would say is try to wake up an hour before you usually do and give yourself some time for a morning routine. Your morning routine is unique to you and your needs.

Decide the night before when you're going to wake up. Most people wake up when they feel like it versus when they decide to or when they should. That's a big productivity killer and obviously if you go to bed tired, you will wake up tired. If you go to bed with a positive attitude and you visualize right before bed, you wake up more energized. Make sure you wake right up. No snooze, because if you hit the snooze button you're literally resisting life. You're resisting actually living. Right after you're physically out of bed, drink a big bottle of water.

One of the things I teach people about productivity is that the biggest trick is deciding what you're going to work on at some point other than in the moment. In the morning, one of the biggest keys is getting clarity and preparing your day, and making sure you're energized and that you're in the right state of mind to be courageous and attack those action plans. You can do this in different ways. You can spark your body with a work out. When I work out in the morning, I'm more alert and aware throughout the day.

After I work out, I review my day. I prepare my day and I prioritize items based on my goals. Once I have my day planned, I like to spark my mind. So whether it's reading a book, listening to a podcast or an audio or video, I'm in such a different state of mind when I put positive vibes in my mind instead of watching the news or focusing on things that aren't going well. Next, I ask myself three questions. What am I excited about for the day? What am I grateful for today? And what am I committed to making happen no matter what? So after I spark my mind, I prioritize and I ask myself those questions. Right there you can bet you're in a better mindset, and you'll be more productive.

It's not so much when you actually wake up that matters. It's that you have purpose in your day and are living it with intention. I know people who wake up at 3:30 a.m. and others who wake up around 10 a.m. That's fine, but you must be conscious of what it is you're doing during the day to make sure you're getting the most out of each day. Some people wake up early and they do their morning routine, but throughout the day they get lethargic or they fail to get things done. So it's almost pointless to wake up early unless you're maximizing the time you have. You don't have to wake up at four or five, but it will give you a good head start. There are a lot of people I've studied who do wake up early because while everyone else is heading to work or sleeping they're getting a head start with inner work so the day goes more productively. It all depends on your goals.

If you have some pretty big goals and you want to build a big business or you want to create an amazing lifestyle, there's a period of time where you'll have to sacrifice. Wake up earlier. Go to bed later. All entrepreneurs have done it. As an entrepreneur seeking success, you can't afford nor have the flexibility to sleep whenever you want.

Pick a morning routine and stick with it for at least ten days. Make sure you spark the body and mind, but figure out a routine that makes you feel energized and ready for the day. If it's not working, then switch it up and try something else. If you stick with it, you'll see the difference in the energy, the clarity, and the confidence you have throughout the day.

Chapter XXII Action Steps:

1. Create your own morning routine and stick to it for at least 10 days.

2. Reflect on how you feel after 10 days. Write down the benefits you experienced. Don't be afraid to try new things until your morning routine is optimal for you and your needs.

XXIII

The Power Of EvE Ratio

Next, I am going to discuss the power of the EvE ratio that I learned from Brian Tracy. I don't think there's a bigger perspective flip that you can have than with this philosophy. I know a lot of people reading this book are already game changers and members of our program, but if you're not then you should check out **www.gamechangersmovement.com**, especially if you want to hear Brian Tracy speak live and ask him questions.

In regards to the EvE ratio, the question I want to ask is: "How much time do you spend on activities that really enhance your life and really move your business forward?" Most people spend their time on entertainment, which is something that has nothing to do with improving their future or building their life.

Essentially, the EvE ratio is the amount of time a person spends on entertainment versus education. According to Brian Tracy, the average person spends 50 minutes on entertainment for every 1 minute spent on education and personal growth. That's a disproportionate amount of time. If you want to find one of the fastest ways to increase your growth and really increase your success in life and business, it's to decrease your ratio for entertainment and increase your ratio for education. It's that simple. Change your ratio and you will change your life. There's nothing else to it.

The first switch I made that had a huge impact in my business and personal success was when I reduced my entertainment and increased my education. I wasn't really into personal development at first. I read *Rich Dad Poor Dad*, but I wasn't taking a lot of action. I thought my energy and ambition would take me places, but I didn't have any real guidance. I didn't know what I was doing, nor did I have the right philosophy. I had entertainment, non-stop. I would go to basketball games, watch TV or a movie, go out with friends, spend time on Facebook, and so on.

Once I got into business and really started shifting my ratio, I started to see real success. Now this may be difficult for a lot of people because most people are used to drowning themselves in entertainment every day of the week. If they have a job they don't like, when they get home, they just want to veg in front of the TV. This adds no real value to you in the long term. Therefore, it is probably not going to help you in the future.

To be clearer, when I refer to entertainment, I refer to any activity where you're turning off your brain and stunting your personal growth. This could include everything from watching TV, blindly surfing the web, going to a sporting event, or taking off for vacation. I'm not saying these are bad, but if your ratio is too tilted towards entertainment, you're never going to get where you want to go. The goal is not to eliminate entertainment; it's to try to identify activities in your life that waste your time or don't add significant value.

In 2009, I really got into personal development and I had the best year of my life. Up to that point, I had never experienced such a positive boost in my income, excitement, relationships, impact, and even the fun I had. My ratio was probably 20 to 80. Instead of watching TV or movies, I spent my time reading and learning. I chose to make that switch to see what it would do for my success, and it just catapulted me to different stratospheres that I hadn't been in before. So I challenge you to make the same switch.

Here is an example. When you think back to the best experiences you had last year, do you immediately remember all those times reading the newspaper or watching Family Guy? Probably not. More often, you're going to remember the things that changed your life in a dramatic way, when you impacted someone, or when you met that amazing mentor. Examples of education are personal growth audios, seminars, mastermind groups, listening to my podcasts, taking a class about something that really intrigues you -- maybe it's marketing, business, economics, education, or anything that supports your growth. The first switch is figuring out how to shift that ratio.

The second switch is enhancing your education with actual action steps that are applicable and consistent. Otherwise, education can easily become another form of entertainment if it's not coupled with bold action. In other words, if you stop watching TV to read a non-fiction book instead, but you never use the information from the book, you've simply entertained your brain and made no progress. So if you don't watch TV and instead read three books, but nothing changes as far as action or results, you might as well watch TV. You have to implement your education for it to be truly effective. It's not easy. I used to be the same way. But the faster you understand this philosophy, the faster you'll succeed, and in this fast paced economy there is no other option but to succeed quickly.

It's necessary to focus on consistent action in one particular area before moving on. People are often obsessed with absorbing a lot of information. You need to simplify that information and make it useable.

That's the single reason why we created the Game Changers program, so people not only have the right action to take and the right strategies with the right network of people, but they have massive accountability. The only way to really get to the next level is to have someone who holds you accountable. You need to have a group of people, a mentor, a coach, or a team to hold you accountable, because, as I said, people get absorbed in these books, but they don't take any action. Knowing that someone is there to push you forward makes you more likely to put what you learn into practice. Information is great, but it's what you do with the information that really matters.

In this second switch, making sure the personal growth is action oriented, that's where a mentor or a new community of people are absolutely necessary for you to take your life to the next level. How do you actually go about finding that new community of people or finding those mentors? Well, ten years ago I'd say it would have been somewhat challenging, but now it's like tying your shoelaces. There's meetup.com, there are mastermind groups in every city, there's the Young Professionals Network, and so many more. Our Game Changers program has some of the most success minded and young, hungry professionals on the planet, and we can help you connect with them. Join programs, go to entrepreneurial events, go to seminars, or talk to professors at your school. You can even talk to business owners in your town and ask them if they know anybody who is young and successful that you can connect with. You can look on LinkedIn for people who have similar interests as you. You can actually go on Twitter and type in what you are passionate about and what you like, and from there find out who's talking about those subjects and connect with them. The possibilities are endless.

Too often, especially as entrepreneurs, we can sometimes isolate ourselves, and that's something that we need to break out of. No one succeeds alone and no one fails alone. There are always people around you, so you've got to make sure they're the right people. And even if you feel alone, there are still some people impacting you. It's crucial to have the right core group around you if you want to succeed in business.

The double-edged sword of personal development is that there's a lot of useful knowledge you can gain, and it either leads to great success or enormous stress and overload. Remember, when you're overwhelmed, you seek distractions. This is the classic case in our society right now, especially with the young generation. We all seem to suffer from analysis paralysis, confusion, overwhelm, and overload. If you're feeling all of those things, there's no way you're going to take the right action. So make sure you pace yourself and only read as much as you can absorb and take action on.

One thing I teach my coaching clients and my members is when you're reading a book, make sure the book is absolutely congruent to your vision and that the information helps you. It's a skill that you want to work on and a trait that you need to develop. To get the most out of books, when you read a chapter, highlight parts that you can apply and take action on before you move on. Then, to really master new information, teach what you learn to others. It's so much easier to retain information when you teach it. Only once you've taken these steps should you move on to the next chapter.

There's so much to do and there's so little time. As you increase your time on personal development, you'll find yourself with a bigger to do list since you'll have more time available because you're more productive. Having too many to do's can be stressful, so you have to be able to prioritize that list and focus on the most effective tasks. How you manage your priorities and create more free time is the key here. If you struggle with using your time efficiently, listen to some time management modules to figure out how to be more effective. There will be a point of stress when you're growing. You'll lose some people who are not growing. You'll feel a little overwhelmed and experience some stress. This is all good because it means you're pushing your limits and once your limits are pushed, they become standards. And those higher standards bring you to a higher level of performance.

I can look at anybody and break down his or her schedule. By looking at their EvE ratio, I can tell you their bank account. I can tell you how they're feeling and if they're making progress or struggling. There are certain things you do that help your future and there are certain things that make you feel good in the moment, but kill your future. So I would challenge you to be careful with what you do, and if you are having fun and enjoying yourself, do it when you deserve it instead of when you feel like it.

Chapter XXIII Action Steps:

1. Evaluate your EvE ratio, and make sure you're aware of how you're spending your time.

2. Commit to lower your entertainment level and increase your education level by at least 20%.

3. Dedicate yourself to learning something new once per month and teach what you learn to others.

XXIV

The "I Don't Have Enough Time" Myth

Personally, one of the things I really take pride in and am passionate about is taking time out of my day to put on my Podcasts because I know how much it's helping young entrepreneurs worldwide. So I'm always up for it and I always make the time. I'm excited to shatter the "I don't have enough time" myth that people grab onto so tightly. Everyone has the same amount of time: me, you, Oprah, Tony Robbins, Michael Jordan, Richard Branson, and Howard Schultz. We all have the same amount of time -- 24 hours in a day. How it's managed is what really separates the wealthy from the poor. How you treat your time separates the successful people from the average.

What you have to do for successful time management is shift your mindset. To help you understand this better, I want to share a few facts. First, it's not the hours you work, it's the work you put into the hours. If you're not even effective from nine to five, what makes you think you're going to be effective after that? Are you really being effective and efficient, focusing on the highest value activities before the others? Secondly, either you're running your weeks or your weeks are running you. 95% of people don't plan ahead. But the 5% who do plan ahead make more than those 95% combined. To be successful, you need to start predetermining and planning out in detail ahead of time what you want to accomplish. You can always get more money, but you can never get more time. And like I said earlier, how time is managed separates the wealthy from the struggling.

There are people who are busier than you with a lot more responsibility getting a lot more done, period. People have been trying to master time management and maximize their time for years. But the truth is, it's not about time at all. It's really about self-management, not time management.

I was working 70 or 80 hours a week but I wasn't strategic or intentional and I went broke. Once I shifted my perspective and understood the concept of becoming more valuable, I made better decisions. I started treating my time wisely, got a mentor, and joined a mastermind group, and that's when things really started shifting dramatically and quickly. I went from working 80 hours to 40 and doubling my results. There are 24 hours in a day and 168 hours in a week. Let's say people spend 52 hours a week sleeping, about 7 ½ a night. You don't need that, especially if you're under the age of 30. What are you doing sleeping past 6 or 7 hours? You have so much energy. Right now is the time to change the game, start movements, build legacies, dominate your companies and do amazing things. So stop sleeping your precious time away. You spend 50 hours a week at school or work. After 52 hours a week sleeping and 50 hours a week at school or work that's 102 hours. Let's say you spent 15 hours a week eating, and 24 hours a week doing nothing, like relaxing, playing video games, watching movies and TV. That's 141 hours! As Jim Rubens says, "Successful and wealthy people have big libraries, poor people have big TVs." I'm not saying don't have a TV, but just make sure you've completed your priorities before you sit down and watch TV.

Now, you could watch 5 more hours of TV and you would still have 18 hours unaccounted for. So after you slept, you worked, you worked out, you went to school, you ate, you watched TV and you relaxed, there's still 18 hours left. So where does the "I don't have enough time" myth come from? There's no truth in that statement. Successful people never say "I don't have enough time". They welcome challenges, they take on more, and they find time to get everything done that is important to them.

When you say you don't have enough time, what you really mean is that you just haven't made it important for you, that you haven't sold yourself on it yet. You need to catch yourself saying, "I don't have enough time", and change it to, "I'm not making enough time" or "It doesn't mean enough to me." Ask yourself why you want to get better at time management. If you don't have a strong enough gut-wrenching reason, then you're not going to get better at it. You're simply going to keep running the same routines you've been running. Is it because you want more time for your kids, more time for loved ones, peace of mind, or more time to train for a marathon? Do you want more time to work on your other business or time to travel? Make your reason to learn time management a good one.

When I was working 80 hours and making a substantial amount of money at 23-years-old, guess what I didn't have that I wanted? Time. I was working, making money, but I didn't have time to enjoy any of my success. That's why I got good at time management. I wanted a different lifestyle, so I studied time-management relentlessly, interviewed the experts, and read 40 books about how to use my time effectively. Now I have both money and time to enjoy it.

You do have enough time. You just have to make time, prioritize, and cut out things that don't matter to you. Then you can work on that tactical-structural part of time management, which is planning your day and preparing and putting things in a schedule.

Protect your time. It's really valuable.

XXV

Tactics To Help You Get The Most Out Of Your Day

What I'm going to talk about next is something that so many people struggle with. So many people are trying to figure out how to handle the topic of time and time management. In order to have a great lifestyle you need to have a grasp on time, and not just time management, but self-management. It's really about how to maximize the time you put into things, in terms of leverage, in terms of partnership, experience, intelligence, and planning. You have to learn this skill if you want to live your dream lifestyle and start creating something that really matters.

Shift from complexity to simplicity. Get rid of all the noise out there and simplify your life. The first step is to write a one-page productivity plan. You need to have one page where you have a vision statement of what your life is going to be like in a year, what your driving purpose or calling is as far as your company vision, and what you want to accomplish by the end of this year. No matter how far away that is, write a vision statement that can guide your life. You want to let your vision guide you, not your current circumstances. Next, write down your top values. What's important to you? What are your principles and values as an entrepreneur?

Write your top five-yearly goals just below your top values. Then, answer the following questions: "Am I living my purpose?" "Am I giving my best daily?" "Am I thinking and acting like a million dollar manager?" Whatever questions mean the most to you. I also want you to include any meaningful quotes that drive and motivate you.

This one page becomes your guiding principle. You stay intentional now. One question I always ask myself is, "How large are my intentions each day?" Your intentions should be to do something magnificent, and they should inspire you so you stay focused and don't procrastinate. The first step to time management is to have a one-page document you can look at to remind you of what you're doing, why you're doing it, and the important things in life. Now I want you to pause and reflect on your week. Figure out how last week went; figure out where you made mistakes, and where you did well. You need to invest in last week's experience to create this week's planning. This is a crucial point. If you want to maximize time management, you have to make sure you're pausing and reflecting and writing a paragraph and thinking about how last week went because, sadly, most people make the same mistakes over and over again. Have you ever had those times, or have you ever heard of people having times where they had a really shitty month, and then the next month is just as shitty? They're like, "Man, I'm having a couple bad months." It's because they never actually paused and reflected on why that month was so bad. Powerful questions are huge. What did you get done last week? What went well? What didn't go well? Where did you waste your time? What are you 100% committed to getting done this week? What are you excited about? What are your top wins from last week? Pausing and reflecting is a huge part of time management mastery.

The next thing you do is predetermine your outcome. Here are the facts: you're either creating your ideal life, or taking what's given and living everybody else's expectations of you -- a guaranteed way to regret things. Therefore, predetermine your week. What are your most valuable priorities? Write down your top three business priorities and your top three personal priorities. Now, you need to make your priorities income-based because you can't survive without an income. Some people are like, "I don't care about money." That's fine. I've done experiments and it is more fun to have money than it is to be broke. If your priority is not to make money, what are you doing? Make that a priority, and make sure you have the business to back that up.

It is also necessary for you to reach out. Who are you committed to connecting to that will help you advance your goals? That's a question you ask while you're planning your week. Who do you need to reach out to that's playing the game at a higher level than you? Then what do you do after you predetermine what you're going to do with your priorities? You have to sell yourself on those priorities. We've talked about this before. Sell yourself on why you need to do those, because if you haven't sold yourself on them, you're not going to do them. Once you have your priorities, you have the people you're going to reach out to and you've sold yourself, then you put them in your schedule. You're going to put in everything you can't change in your schedule. The "non-negotiables" like work, school, workouts, whatever you do that's non-negotiable to you, put those in first. After that, you put in accountability systems like results rituals. What are you going to do week after week that has been proven to get results? For me, after a couple months of my business, I knew what created results and made me money, and what didn't. So I made sure that every week I had those things in my schedule. That's why I was one of the most consistent managers of all time. I don't say that to brag, but I say it to impress upon you that it's because I put results rituals in my schedule. Put time limits in your schedule for each item. Put time limits, because as time decreases, intensity increases.

Do everything you can to get yourself in the zone. The zone is the place where nothing can bug you or distract you. I assure you, you'll be three times more productive, more efficient, and more effective. Get yourself in that zone as much as you can.

After you put things in your schedule, then it's all about protecting your time. Here's the problem. We're going to seek out distractions when we become overwhelmed. If you don't protect your time, and you don't put things in your schedule, then you're going to become overwhelmed. And you already know when you're overwhelmed, instantly you're going to seek out and try to find distractions. Figure out what's killing your productivity momentum. You need to make sure you've actually defined your distractions, and you've taken care of them beforehand. If you don't have a plan to prevent interruptions, your plans will always be interrupted.

There are two more ways to protect your time. First, be aware of where you've wasted time in the past. Second, get used to saying the word "no". Stop trying to please everybody. Mediocrity does that. Mediocre people do that, but not driven people like you. Get used to saying no. What made Apple successful, according to Steve Jobs, was everything he said no to, not what he said yes to. And the moment you try to please everybody, the person you don't please is you.

Once you protect your time, you've got to be present. Wherever you are, be there. Be observant in the present moment. Base what you do off your standards, instead of your emotions, like I've said many times. Focus, focus, focus on what you've already pre-determined. What this does is it reminds you that when you were making your schedule, you were in an intelligent mindset. So four days later, when you look at your schedule, and notice you have a workout to do but you don't feel like it, you'll catch yourself and you'll do your workout. If you don't make a schedule, in the middle of the week, you're not always going to feel like what you planned. But if you actually have a schedule to back it up, and you remember why, then you're going to stay focused. In this way, your schedule is a reflection of your integrity. So stand true to yourself and honor your schedule.

Time management is about seizing each day. I was talking to Eric Thomas a couple months ago, and I asked him how he does all the events he does. He has almost a hundred million views on YouTube. He speaks to the NBA, and to top athletes. He has a family, a son and a daughter. His motto is: "I just seize each day." If you're making the most of each day, the weeks and months will take care of themselves.

Chapter XXV Action Steps:

1. Make self-management your top priority. Write down your top goals for the year and the reasons you want to achieve them.

2. Create simple actions steps to achieve your goals.

3. Keep a schedule and honor what you pencil in.

XXVI

Six Tips To Double Your Productivity

Let's start talking about productivity. I've given a lot of speeches and talks on this subject, and because of that I've received hundreds of e-mails, phone calls, text messages, and Facebook messages about productivity and how to get more out of your day, life, and business. So I've got a lot to share on this subject.

The way I define productivity is the output and working towards a productive life -- towards a life that you're truly proud of -- which lets you have flexibility, freedom, and joy. Being productive is working towards a productive life where you're doing what you love with flexibility, freedom, and choices. Whatever can help you get there, whatever can help you be more efficient, is what productivity is, as long as it's focused on moving you towards a better life.

I have a lot of productivity tips that I've gained over the years. The first tip is refusing interference. I do fight distraction in my own life and I teach the teams and people I work with the same. Everyone's fighting for your attention from articles, commercials, parents, friends, teachers, businesses, marketing agencies, and people on social media. There are too many people stealing all your attention. Don't be so generous in giving it to them. You need to protect your focus and figure out what your distractions are and get rid of them. There are certain things that come up habitually, every time you try to get something done, that you might not notice. Maybe you check your email or search the internet, or maybe you check your text messages while you're working. Think about what's interfering with your productivity, and take care of those before they come up.

I read a while back that Special Forces on a military mission are kept in isolation from other teams and they're denied access to TVs, newspapers, the Internet, and so forth. Why? To protect their focus so they can deliver perfection on their goals. Distraction is really the greatest thief of all time. Time is a non-renewable resource. Once you're distracted, you can't get that time back. It's not helping you at all to move towards a better business or in having more flexibility and freedom.

Tip number two: Stop multitasking. I catch myself doing this, but I try not to. I set timers. I make sure that before I ever open my computer I know exactly what I'm doing online. If you just open up your computer, you're not going to know what to get done. You're going to catch yourself on Facebook, Twitter, or LinkedIn, before you even get anything important done. They say the immature mind hops from task to task, but the mature mind stays on one task until completed at an excellent level. I think a lot of people are not present in the work or activities in front of them. I see people in the airport checking their phones and Twitter feeds. I see a lot of taxi drivers reviewing their emails while driving. A huge competitive advantage falls to the one in one hundred performers with the brilliance to develop the skill of becoming focused on the one thing in front of them. This is truly a game-changing move. Stop multitasking.

Build rituals of productivity which are things you do every week that are proven to get results. I work in 90-minute cycles. There's a ton of science confirming that's the best way to complete important tasks. I'll do two or three different cycles where I'll work in 90 minute increments, fully focused, with something that's already intentionally planned. Then I'll take a five to ten minute break. I'll walk around the block, I'll do some push-ups, or I'll watch a video to get my mind off of the task. Then I'll re-focus and get back on task for the next 90 minutes.

I usually turn my technology off for 60 plus minutes per day and focus on doing my most important work. When I'm doing my most important work in those 90 minutes, I'll turn my technology off or on silent. If you know me personally, then you know I don't really ever answer my phone unless it's planned. Those who know me know that I have to call them back on my own time. There was a guy, who didn't answer his phone for years; he only called people back on his own time. That's such a great way to be productive, to do work when you want to work, and call people back when you have decided to. You're not letting other people run your agenda. This is a big one. If I can give you one tip that'll make a big difference, this is it: turn all of your notifications off on your phone. There are 19 and 20 year olds who are trying to be productive. They put on Facebook "Yeah, I'm the next game changer. I'm crushing it." But they're broke and they have 42 distractions per hour. I know that's happening. So turn off all emails, Facebook, Twitter, Vine, anything that would send you a push notification. I have no notifications. If my phone sat next to me all day, I'd hear nothing until I wanted to. That's huge. All productive people do that. The people who really don't mind being interrupted never get anything important done. Data says that workers are interrupted every 11 minutes, and distractions really destroy productivity. So learn to protect your time, and say no to those interruptions. Better yet, take care of them before they come up.

I try to get a lot of work done before I start hanging around family. It's hard to be productive when you're with your family because they distract you. It's tough to do. So I try to get everything done beforehand so I can fully enjoy them and be present when we spend time together.

End procrastination. Many of us will procrastinate by waiting for the ideal conditions to get big things done. You've got to stop waiting for perfect conditions. One of the things billionaires do that most don't is they focus on experiments instead of perfection. You need to make sure that you're experimenting and that you're trying things when you're not fully ready. You might not know everything or exactly what to do, but so what? You'll figure it out along the way. You'll adjust course and adapt as you go. So look for experiments, not perfection. If you take action, even when you don't feel like it, you're going to end procrastination. One thing I do, if I'm thinking about doing something, I just do it right away. I don't even let time go by. If I'm thinking about it, and I know I should do it, I do it immediately. Stop putting off what you know you need to do.

A lot of productive people set to-do lists, but those who play at a world-class level they set not to-do lists as well. They set lists of "What am I not going to do?" I'm not going to check Facebook, I'm not going to sleep in, I'm not going to answer my phone when I don't want to. Steve Jobs said that what helped Apple really be Apple was not so much what they chose to build, but all the projects they chose to ignore. Making a stop-doing list is really important in killing procrastination and you won't be resentful about doing things you don't want to or shouldn't do.

Don't check your email first thing in the morning. It puts you in a bad mood and you need to do something more productive. Do your hardest task first, after your morning routine, of course. I try not to check my e-mail until 10 a.m. If I check it beforehand, I get caught up in it and I waste time. Don't check your email until later in the day. Check your email two times a day, and respond during those set times. There's a thing called touch it once, where when you see an email, touch it once. Either file it, respond to it, or delete it. The worst thing you can do is put it off until later. Then they just pile up and up. If you want to be productive, get it done right away. Respond, file, or delete it immediately.

Schedule every day of your week every Sunday morning. A plan kind of relieves you of the torment of choice. It restores focus, and provides energy as well. I've done this for years now. The trick to productivity is deciding what you're going to do at some point other than in the moment. Then practice that high-value work over and over, until it's natural, habitual, and automatic. That's what making a schedule on Sunday does. It destroys the torment of choice. I try to pre-determine my outcome for the week first.

Chapter XXVI Action Steps:

1. Use these productivity tips in your day.

2. Start planning your week and your time on Sunday.

3. Follow through on action items in your schedule.

4. You may notice I keep repeating a few action steps. I am doing this on purpose because what I'm sharing is crucial for you to be successful.

XXVII

Six More Tips To Double Your Productivity

Earlier, I offered several productivity tips, some ways that people can really live the life they've always dreamed of, the life they want, and working towards something that provides freedom, joy, and flexibility. If you've gotten this far without mastering any of the tips that I've previously mentioned in this book, you're going to fall victim to information overload, which is the reason why 99% of people are excited and motivated, yet broke. They have ambition but no goals and no achievements. So, if you haven't mastered any of my earlier points, stop reading. Stop reading right now and go to the previous chapter, write those productivity tips down and work on them one by one until you feel that you've mastered them. You don't need 16 tips at once. You need to master one before you master the next one. I want to make that point because if you've read my book this far and have mastered my various tips and your bank account is not stacked right now, there's a problem. I'm not joking. Reach out to me and I'll help you. If you haven't joined GameChangers and you haven't stacked your bank account within the last couple of months of following my advice, there really is an issue and it might be holding you back. It might even continue over the next couple of years because we're defined by our habits. So I'm telling you, you need to go back and read the ones that you know you need help with, and plan on mastering those because mastery is the highest form of accomplishment. It's not necessarily about the information you're gathering; it's all about the implementation you're doing. So let's get back to some more productivity tips.

Get in the zone. Here's the problem -- we're addicted to distractions. Most people allow themselves to get distracted because distraction is addictive. Our brain loves this because every time we get distracted, our brain releases endorphins and dopamine, which are like the feel-good drugs, according to Robin Sharma. He says when we get distracted our brain gets happy. So people like distractions. They like their email, text messages, social media and the new game "Angry Birds." There are so many games! You have to realize that the person who invented that game is a millionaire and he doesn't play it. People who play it are broke.

So when you see a new email or text message pop up on your phone, ignore it. You are three times more productive when you're in the zone and you only get in the zone when you zero in and concentrate. Everyone has been in the zone in the past, right? Whether it's in sports or writing a book or on an assignment and 40 minutes have gone by and you didn't even notice. That's the zone. You're thinking more intelligently. You're really expressing your genius. You are completely focused.

It takes at least twenty minutes to get back in the zone. But most people are already distracted again before the twenty minutes are up, so they're never actually working at their peak. Remember, focus is actually more important than intelligence. And I'm sure you know there are a lot of broke geniuses and some millionaires who are not that intelligent, but they can focus on things that bring high-value results and add value to the marketplace. So get in the zone as much as you can during the week. If you want to spend more time with your family, and go out more and have fun, get in the zone more during your workweek. And before I get off that topic, a great book that dives even further into this is *The Rise of Superman.* It's one of my favorite books. I'm reading through it a second time already and it is one I'd highly suggest you invest in.

Besides getting in the zone, you need to make sure you sell yourself. I know I've said this already, but I want to expand a bit so you really learn this. The reason why a lot of people can't focus consistently is because they haven't actually sold themselves on what they're doing. By "sold" I mean you've cut out every alternative. You know the importance of why you're doing what you're doing and the purpose of the outcome. If you procrastinate on something, it's because you just haven't sold yourself on getting it done yet.

For example, let's take someone who's in school. You have a big test coming up and you have three weeks to study and you don't sell yourself on why you should study right away, so you don't study until the last second. You're going to develop a habit of being a procrastinator. Everything you do and every deadline you have to meet, you'll wait until the last-minute. And that's how you live your life until someone gives you a reality-check or something happens and you aren't successful at what you're doing because of that habit. But let's say you sold yourself on being the one out of a hundred students who studies the first week and studies relentlessly, morning and night to where you have it down and you're going to get an A no matter what they throw at you. And then the last two weeks of the test, you can chill out and have fun. You can go home for a week and see your family before finals when everyone else is going crazy in dead week. If you sell yourself on that enough, you're going to do it.

That's why it's so important to sell yourself. If you haven't sold yourself on who you're with, you're probably going to break up eventually. If you haven't sold yourself on why you should quit smoking, why you should not drink, or why you should not party when you're not satisfied with your results, you're going to keep doing it. So figure out what you need to sell yourself on and don't get yourself involved in anything unless you're fully committed to it. When someone reaches out and wants me to do a podcast, I have to be sold on it. They have to have a big enough audience. It has to make sense for me because I really value my time. So I have to sell myself on what's going on and what is in front of me in order to do it. I suggest you do the same.

Show up charged. I strongly recommend spending twenty to thirty minutes in the morning exercising, no matter what, and drinking a ton of water because that will start your day charged. We talked about morning routines, but how you show up is exactly how your entire day goes. So if you show up with energy and strength, you'll be more productive. A morning routine is crucial to creating a great day, and all successful people start their day in a powerful way. Do your actions and thoughts in the morning set you up for a winning day or just another day? Showing up charged is a great way to be more productive and effective.

Another productivity tip is getting good at reverse engineering. Engineers working with technology startups are masterful at taking a competitor's product and breaking it apart, piece-by-piece. Engineers are good at reverse engineering and figuring out the components needed to make a world-class product. We need to do the same thing with our own lives. Truly productive people do the same thing with their most valuable opportunities. They know how to reverse back to the final result and they can get back to what they need to do monthly or weekly, and gain clarity around their action steps that are focused on the end result. Therefore, if you're really aware, you will reverse-engineer this big goal into a series of small and actionable steps. Then you put those into a one-to-two page execution plan. It's worked for me for years and it will work for you as well. So get really good at breaking things down -- big goals into smaller action steps, focus on the end result, put all the pieces together in between, and then put it on paper so you can see the plan.

You must practice productivity. The more you practice what you know, the better you get. There's a state of passively knowing something and then there's a level of performance you attain when you consistently practice what you know. For example, I love basketball. I play it all the time. Professional basketball players know how to shoot a free-throw, but they still shoot them every single day, over and over and over again, because they're committed to reaching the highest level of performance. So practice what you know over and over again because this is going to build your muscle memory, meaning that if you practice a technique relentlessly, a time will eventually come where you can perform it swiftly and unconsciously. The same applies to your productivity. You need to practice doing work that matters. Practice sitting in one place for ninety minutes at a time focused on one, single result. Practice running rituals in an elite performance routine that will lift you into the class of achievement that very few people attain. Because as you already know, genius isn't so much about genetics as it is about work ethic, sheer perseverance, and consistency. So take the time to examine your own life and incorporate these strategies and principles into your daily routines. These tips, if applied, will help transform your productivity, performance, and lifestyle as well. And remember, it's not what you know, it's what you do and the actions you take with regards to what you know -- that's where the real power of change and transformation lives. So let's all operate at a world-class level.

XXVIII

How To Put A Stop To Your Momentum Killers

In this chapter, I would like to talk about something that has made a profound difference in my life, and the lives of a lot of people I work with as well.

Here's what people don't understand or think about. There are things that are happening to you that are killing your momentum. So my question is, what has killed your momentum in the past? Let's think about it. When things are going well and when things are rocking, you have momentum. But then something ruins your momentum. Most people don't take the time to recognize what their momentum killers are, so every year, the same things are killing their momentum.

This is what I do for people that I work with, and I want you to do this too. Think about the last 12 months. What are the two or three top things that have killed your momentum? It can be your motivation, it can be your circle of influence, it can be the grass is greener syndrome where you always think there is something better to do than what you're doing now, or it could even be sleeping in.

You might be wondering why momentum is so important in your life.

The scariest thing in life and business is momentum. The second scariest thing is lack of momentum. So why we talk about this is because if you have a lack of momentum, it's extremely hard to get motivated, to get out of bed, to stay focused, to work late, or to wake up early. But if you can take care of those distractions and momentum breakers before they come up and put prevention plans in place, there's no limit to how big you can build your momentum. And with momentum on your side, you become more consistent.

The next step is creating a plan to stop those momentum killers and get your life going again. First you have to ask yourself, what's killing your momentum and productivity? Then, write it down. And let me give you some examples. Distractions, social media, your notifications, multitasking, your environment, lack of planning or priorities, procrastination, sleep -- ultimately, you have to figure out what your top three are, and then figure out how to take care of those before they come up. The first step is being aware of your momentum killers.

For example, let’s say your momentum killer is multitasking. You get caught up in numerous projects at the same time. Therefore, you can’t give your full attention to any of them. I know one person who has set up some systems and elaborate task lists for every single project he has. That way, he has everything systematized so he knows what steps need to happen in order to move that project forward. And then he can also create another one or two action steps that would ensure that even when things are going well, he doesn’t fall back on his old habits. I can't come up with the action steps for him, just like I can’t do it for you. You have to pull it out of yourself by just becoming aware. The simple fact of becoming aware is going to put you ahead of most people because most people, when you look at their years, this year is the same as last year, or sometimes worse. Few people grow every single year. If someone doesn't know what's killing their momentum and they're not aware of it, what do you think keeps happening year after year? That same thing keeps popping up and it keeps killing their momentum over and over and over again.

We're going to seek out distractions when we become overwhelmed. So if you're overwhelmed, you're going to find a way to get distracted. That's why you have to kill these distractions before they come up. Figure out your momentum killers and the distractions, and then create a prevention plan so you don't get distracted again.

So here's another example – cell phones. Turn off all your notifications. That's killing your productivity. If you want to have mediocre income and you want to produce only average work, get distracted all the time. So turn off notifications. When you're doing work, when you're planning a meeting, when you're talking to somebody, put your phone away. Have it on silent. I basically put my phone on 'do not disturb' or completely off for most of the day. You don't want other people running your agenda. You don't want other people controlling your schedule. You want to be ultimately in control of your schedule, lifestyle, and your business. So, have phone calls on your own time. Call people back when you want to call them back. Of course, make it prompt if it's important, but don't get run by your distractions because either you're running your days or your days are running you.

When you take care of your distractions before they come up, and when you have a plan to prevent your interruptions, your plans will never be interrupted. That's the key to preventing your momentum from being halted and staying focused on what matters and getting in the zone versus being distracted all the time.

Chapter XXVIII Action Steps:

1. Start being mindful about your momentum killers. Simply become aware of when you get distracted. Write those times down.

2. Use your list and make a firm commitment to stop letting one of those momentum killers happen.

3. Put a plan in place to prevent that momentum killer from interrupting your important work.

XXIX

How To Differentiate Yourself

For this chapter, I want to really focus on how to differentiate from everybody else around you. I want to teach you how to figure out what makes you different and how to start dominating your competition versus competing.

You might be wondering, why is this so important for an entrepreneur? Well there's hundreds of thousands of applicants out there, and most people are just a drop in a sea of applicants hoping to get hired or hoping to start their own business. They simply don't realize there are 150 other people, or 150,000 other people who are just like them with the same resume experience. So you have to differentiate yourself if you want to actually build a great lifestyle, which is what this book is all about.

The first step you need to take when differentiating yourself is to figure out a very powerful why. No matter where you are, you can always take it up a notch. The possibilities are endless when you strengthen your "why" and come up with compelling reasons. So you need to really focus on coming up with reasons why you want to be different, why you want a better lifestyle, why you want more income, why you want to be a leader, and why you don't want to be like the majority. I did some case studies and one of my case studies stated that over 60% of college students can't find work in their field after college. And the scary thing is the average price of college is skyrocketing while the average income a student makes after graduation is at an all-time low. *The Huffington Post* reported tuition is up 27% over the past 4 years, yet students can't find jobs after they graduate. Therefore, you need to have a very strong why, a reason why you don't want to be a statistic like that. When you have a why that's strong, you'll start searching for and finding a way to differentiate yourself. It starts with having a compelling reason because, as you know, if you don't have a reason why you're doing it, you're just going to be average like most people.

Right now there are so many young professionals who are desperately searching for a career that's within their chosen field or students hoping and praying to find a job once they graduate. And to be honest, many of them probably won't. People need to start creating their own jobs, and start creating their own destiny instead of hoping someone else will see them and decide to hire them. I have friends who are top performing students. They are brilliant when it comes to school smarts, and yet they're working at car rental places or they're working at retail stores. Not that these are bad jobs, but they are bad jobs if you want a wealthy lifestyle, and you're past the age of 25. I see that every day, and it's because they don't have a strong enough "why" to get out of the rut they're stuck in.

You've got to share your "why" and how you've differentiated yourself. You've got to focus on your strengths first, and learn how to delegate your weaknesses. If anyone seriously tells someone to focus on their weaknesses, they haven't really experienced peak performance or a great lifestyle yet. The idols we respect and we all know, have gotten to greatness by focusing on what they're good at and their strengths. What do you see yourself doing if you got a million dollars tomorrow that you would still want to do today? The goal is to be so good at your strengths that it propels you to stand out, and of course everybody loves doing what they're good at, so it makes work even more enjoyable.

Figure out your strengths, start crafting your dream team, and find those people who can complement your weaknesses. One thing our Game Changers program focuses on is how to maximize your strengths and use those strengths to become the best at what you do. To differentiate, you need to focus on habits as opposed to inspiration. Inspiration's needed to create some action, but it's your habits that are ultimately going to define the success or failure of those actions.

After a lot of seminars, only five percent of the people actually use what they've learned. It's because inspiration is short term, and it feels good in the moment, but it doesn't last past the activity producing it. So you need to focus on shifting habits, gaining a better perspective, and interrupting bad thought patterns instead of just relying on inspiration. One way to differentiate is by focusing on doing something daily that's congruent with your strengths, not just being inspired or having spurts of inspiration randomly.

In another case study I found, 71% of people hate what they do and are actively disengaged at work. I was shocked when I read this. Finding something you can see yourself doing and enjoying is another way you can really differentiate yourself. If you can schedule and prioritize based on what matters, based on what gets results, based on what the economy or the marketplace is in demand for, you're going to differentiate yourself at a very high level.

For me, emotional resilience is an important one, so I want to quickly touch on how you go about developing more of it. The biggest key to emotional resilience is through mental toughness. Mental toughness is taking more risks, and building bigger goals, so you can go through more challenges and failures in order to strengthen your perspective and experience. Emotional resilience, like mental toughness, comes from what you take on, who you are around, and how you deal with challenges. It's taking on more and being aware of how you're responding to the challenges, to the urgency, and to the pressure. Companies ask you what you do when nothing goes your way, and if you can answer that in a wise and intelligent fashion, they know you're the real deal and have what it takes to succeed.

If you really want to differentiate, do the opposite of most people. This is a killer strategy for those who want to improve their lives. Go beyond what is expected and do the unexpected. Do something different. Stretch your mind and comfort zone and make your own way. Forge a new path. The greatest companies ever created were brought about by doing something different than everybody else. Don't be like everybody else. No one wants to be typical. Start doing things differently. If everybody's going to school and doing this, don't do that. Maybe go to school, but start a movement at school, or do something different that makes you stand out that other people don't want to do, because it's too risky. That's how you become different.

Chapter XXIX Action Steps:

1. Write down all the unique qualities that make you different. Start with personal characteristics and then go right into professional characteristics.

2. Do something different tomorrow. Make it small if you aren't ready for a risk.

3. Continue to challenge yourself to do things differently for the next 30 days.

XXX

Building A Dynamic Sales Team

Next, I'd like to discuss leadership and how I built a dynamic sales team by being the best leader I could be. There are really two types of people. There are leaders, and then there are followers -- that's it. There is no other type of person so I'm taking a wild guess that if you're reading this, you want to be a leader or you already know you are a leader.

As part of my leadership transformation, I went through a lot of struggles and a lot of growing pains leading a team because I wasn't really developing myself. Leadership isn't someone's position or hierarchy in a company, and leadership has nothing to do with titles. Leadership is not about telling people what to do and it has nothing to do with the personal attributes you were born with. Leadership is not management. Simply having a title doesn't make you a leader. If you have hierarchy or you're above somebody and you are in a managerial role, that doesn't mean people will follow you. They may because they have to, but even then, that's not the best way to lead.

If a title doesn't make a leader, then what does? For example, John C. Maxwell says, leadership is influence. People *choose* to follow you versus *have* to follow you. Leadership is influence. A real leader is not someone who can develop the most followers; a real leader is someone who can develop the most leaders. They're developing other people who can change the game and really lead a team of people to excellence, and not just teach them how to follow. Leadership is the ability to translate vision into reality. Now, as we look into the next century, leadership will be those who empower others, according to Bill Gates. Leadership is empowering others, and being the best you can be so you can help others.

When you lead a team of people, there are very important principles and philosophies you have to follow if you want maximum influence and impact. The first one is standards versus emotions. I already talked a little bit about this more in a success sense, but this is in terms of leadership. When leaders show emotion, show they're tired or hungry or that they are stressed, they instantly lose respect from people around them. You can't really tell if a good leader is having a bad day. Those following me knew when I had a good day, when I had a bad day, or when I was hungry, and I wondered why people weren't listening to or respecting me. Now I know it was because I wasn't really showing them how to be a strong and courageous leader. Start focusing on having standards and principles as a leader. Don't show weakness. You want to make sure you're the one who stays level-headed because people want to follow you and come to you for advice. As a leader, you are an example to your team and the people around you.

Never fear people. When you fear people, you give up your power and you start caring about what people think of you. The best leaders in the world don't fear people and they don't care what people think about them. A leader has to be super-strong in his or her vision and continue to promote that vision regardless of what others think. Leaders don't need to go back for feedback. They are so strong with who they are that the vision they promote attracts the right people. I learned that the hard way. It wasn't until I had a firm vision that was congruent with who I was that I started attracting the right people.

Instead of just telling people what to do or sharing the vision, I learned to teach and inspire people. You want to teach people how to think and how to be independent. You want to teach people how to be future oriented, how to be problem solvers, and self-sufficient. Your followers shouldn't always need you. I told all my best sales reps and managers and executive assistants that after a year with me they wouldn't need me as much anymore because they were going to learn how to be the best on their own and start their own teams and organizations. That got them very excited because they knew I trusted them to do their best. If they are dependent on you, you're always going to have to be there for them. If they always come to you for advice and you don't teach them how to solve problems, they're going to always come to you. Leading people by inspiring and encouraging them is very effective and will help you reach your goals.

As a leader, you have to keep growing. I always try to grow and become better. It's not always an automatic process, it's not a destination; it's a daily thing. Realize that you're always leading and people are always watching you. I am continuously trying to grow by reading books, listening to podcasts, talking to my mentors, and really staying ahead of my game. Not only do I always have access to the answer, but I can tell people where to find the answer so they can go figure it out on their own. Always encourage the people you lead to think, problem-solve, and grow by being an example.

How you do anything is how you do everything. Leadership's about what you do when no one's watching. The year that I had a breakthrough was in 2009. I was always studying and figuring out how to be better at my business and how to lead people to a higher level. No one was watching, so when all the other leaders and managers were out partying or watching TV, I was actually absorbing myself in leadership, studying John C. Maxwell, studying Seth Godin, and reading about Steve Jobs. What do you do when no one's watching? Do you check out or do you use that time to improve?

If you cut a corner in one area of your life it's going to carry on into another area. So if you sleep in a little bit, you're going to eat that pizza that you shouldn't eat because you're on a diet. You eat that pizza and you're going to be late for a meeting. If you're late, you're not going to turn in your assignment on time, and so on. A great leader is always on point. They do everything to the best of their ability without cutting corners. That makes an exceptional leader. Here's an example: Larry Bird. He would shoot a thousand free throws a day. I don't think he missed a day for 15 years. He was one of the best shooters of all time. Do you think that everyone was watching him when he was throwing free throws at his house or at the gym? Nope. When they did see him, he was in the big highlights, right, and in the big games. You didn't see the hundreds of thousands of hours on the back end. It's what you do when no one's watching that really makes you an exceptional leader.

There are a few attributes that are important to express and show as a leader. One is self-control. A man who cannot really control himself cannot control others. Self-control sets the example for the followers about how to behave. A successful leader must have plans that he knows will work and are backed up by strategic thinking and results. A leader can't move by guessing or hoping, but with definite plans that are backed up by data, facts and confidence. If a leader is wary of his plans, so will everyone else be wary.

Chapter XXX Action Steps:

1. Use these leadership principles in your own business and life. Start small and work your way towards emulating them all as your confidence increases.

2. If you're cutting corners or only doing enough to get by, start giving 100% to all you do for 7 days. See if you can feel and see the difference giving your all makes.

3. If you are leading others now, make sure that you are inspiring and encouraging them to be their best by being your best.

XXXI

How To Boost Your Circle Of Influence

I'm very excited about discussing our next topic, the Circle of Influence. This is such a huge, important tip for everybody, but especially for entrepreneurs. I want to explain why this is so important and then give you action steps to boost your circle.

Let's start out by just defining what I mean by circle of influence. Circle of Influence is the people that you surround yourself with the most. Think about this circle as your dream team. The best teams have the best people with the best coach facilitating. Everyone has a team and the people on the team determine their success in the future. A Circle of Influence is who you associate with the most, who is in your network, and who you can reach out to when you need help in reaching your goals.

Why is this circle of influence such an important thing? There was a study where they asked 1,000 of the top sales professionals in the U.S. in international marketing what the strongest reason and predictor of their sales success was in the past. The first predictor was their relationship skills. The second predictor was their social capital -- who they knew. The top 1% of income earners have the highest social capital. Relationships are going to be the number one key to your success, without a question. As an entrepreneur or a sales professional, building relationships is a key activity that's not just fun, but is also critical to your personal growth and business development.

Most people set goals. But here's what they don't do: they don't ask who they need in their circle to reach those goals. Fifty percent of your goal setting is what your goals are and how you're going to get there, but 50% should also be who you need to connect with, build relationships with, add value to, and reach out to, to help you get to your goals. If you hang around five confident people, you'll eventually be the sixth. If you hang out with five intelligent people, you will eventually become the sixth. If you hang out with five millionaires, you'll eventually become the sixth. It's inevitable. But if you hang out with five average people, what's going to happen? You'll eventually be the sixth. Or hang out with five alcoholics, what happens? You're the sixth. So let me give you a few benefits of creating an amazing circle of influence.

The first benefit is shared knowledge. Networking is great for sharing knowledge and ideas. And whether it's asking for feedback or discussing your point of view, it can help you expand your perspective and allow you to see things from someone else's perspective. It's also likely that within a group, or if you're connecting with people that are at a higher level than you, you'll have an opportunity to learn and avoid some of the common pitfalls they've experienced. Shared knowledge is essential.

Another benefit is more opportunities. It's natural, and somewhat obvious, that networking is going to create opportunities, but the thing you will not know is when and how they're going to develop or where they're going to come from. I met a guy a couple of months ago and I just wanted to help him out. What's exciting is I asked him, "Hey, do you know anyone in Hawaii who would want me to speak?" He said, "Oh yeah, some top leaders are there and they would love to have you come and speak. It'll be amazing." Now I have a speech booked in Hawaii speaking to over sixty entrepreneurs just because I met this one person. There are all these different connections and available resources to you when you elevate your circle of influence.

It's also important to increase your income and influence. Now I'm getting a lot of interviews booked with some very successful people because I know other successful people. It's called "Attaching Celebrity." Remember, you're not just gaining exposure to the people you're communicating with, but you're building connections with their network as well. So if someone they know has a need that matches your business, or if they really feel you're genuine and love what you do, they'll make a connection.

One of the best relationship builders I've ever met is John Ruhlan. He's connecting with so many amazing people. I had a meeting with Michael Simmons, who is one of the top editors for Forbes Magazine, just because John said, "Hey, Peter's really big on entrepreneurship, he loves helping young entrepreneurs, and he has a movement that's one of the premier training programs right now for young professionals. I want you to meet him." And now we have a connection. Your circle of influence increases your influence and your income as well, and it's a big part of business.

People always ask me how I went from broke and stressed in my company to breaking a lot of big records. I cut my learning curve in half. One way to learn is to do something right after you've already done it wrong the first time, so you've already learned from the mistakes. Trial and error is a common way to learn. But in order to gain a real benefit, where you can cut your learning curve in half, is learning from other people's experiences. I love Mark Cuban's story, and one of my favorite quotes from him is, "I learned how to become wealthy because I asked the right questions when I was broke." When you learn from other people, you cut your learning curve in half, it elevates your game, and you can get to your goals quicker.

Being visible and getting noticed is a pretty big benefit of networking. By regularly attending business and social events, young entrepreneur groups, BNI groups, and seminars, you can build your reputation as a knowledgeable, reliable source. You don't want to be like everybody else in your industry. You want to figure out what differentiates you, remember? You want to be the leading authority or the expert in your field. When you have amazing connections, it raises your profile.

The final benefit of having a great circle of influence is it lowers stress and raises awareness. When you regularly connect with this circle of influence, you talk to people who have been through what you're going through. Not only will this help increase your confidence, it will also lower your stress level because they'll tell you exactly how to handle it based on their faults and mistakes.

I like to connect to and associate with likeminded people who are playing the game at a very high level. Your circle of influence is so important and, as a young entrepreneur, you need to spend some time building your circle of influence.

I would challenge you to re-evaluate who you spend time with. Figure out the five people you spend the most time with and write down how they are influencing you. People are either holding you accountable or letting you off the hook. They either make you feel amazing or make you feel inferior. They either encourage you or put you down. They either challenge your thinking and inspire you or make you feel dumb and de-motivated. There's no in-between. So figure out who you spend time with and determine who your biggest growth friends are. Once you write down your five growth friends, start spending more time with them. If you don't have a lot of growth friends, then figure out whom you could add to your life, or to your network, to help you grow. And then maintain those friends.

Next, write down people who currently drag you down and limit your time with them. When you have a goal, ask, "Who can help me? Who can I connect with? Who is just as good at this as an expert is? Or, who can I connect with that has already mastered this?" Asking these questions will make a big impact on your successes.

XXXII

FINAL WORDS

While you still have a lot of years to live, be sure to make some time for reaching your dreams. Start working toward your goals now. Don't keep putting things off until it's too late. Tell yourself each day that *now matters*, and realize it's not always about you but those you inspire. Be intentional with your life because that's when you'll feel the most alive, the most resourceful, and the most creative. The more you conform to society and others expectations, the greater your chance of regret. You must consciously choose a new self-image and life. Fight to forge it into existence by consistently aligning your thoughts and behaviors to make it so. I want to thank you for sharing this journey with me. It's time for you to create an exceptional lifestyle and do business on YOUR terms.

I appreciate you.

I want you to stay in the know: Follow me on Twitter @PeterVoogd23 and friend me on Facebook **www.facebook.com/PeterVoogd23**. Also please like my fan page @ **www.facebook.com/PeterJVoogd**. As a thank you for purchasing *"The Entrepreneur Blueprint to Massive Success"* and taking action to start living life on YOUR terms I've assembled a series of valuable tools you can use to help you maximize your entrepreneurial experience and overall productivity. I assure you this will better content than what most have paid thousands for.

Sure, I could have offered you some BS special report or free e-book like most 'online marketers,' but I'd rather give you something practical and proven that will help you move your business forward and help you become the most productive person you know ASAP.

You can claim these amazing free tools at **www.TheEntrepreneurBreakthrough.com**. Enjoy and keep us posted with all your success.

There are two types of people in this world. Those who will do whatever it takes to succeed...and everybody else. Choose wisely.

Peters Most Valuable Resources:

www.TheEntrepreneurBreakthrough.com — Free deep dive training focused on Doubling Your Productivity, Increasing Your Income, and Creating More Flexibility and Autonomy Than Ever Before. $97 Blueprint included as well.

www.GameChangersMovement.com — The premier networking community for Ambitious Entrepreneurs, Professionals, and Game Changers. As featured on Entrepreneur.com, Huffington Post, Business Insider, Inc., MSN, Yahoo, and many other international publications.

www.YoungEntrepreneurLifestyle.com — One of iTunes top podcasts focused on creating a lifestyle business and living life on YOUR terms. We are known for having better content than most pay thousands for.

Other books by Peter Voogd

6 Months to 6 Figures: *The fastest way to go from where you are to where you wanna be"*— **In this book** Peter walks you through step by step the fastest and most effective ways to maximize your income and reach the 6 figure mark as an Entrepreneur. This book will help you create a quantum change in the results you enjoy in your personal and professional life. For more information, please visit **6FiguresBook.com**.

"Peter Voogd inspires us to re-think everything we've learned about Entrepreneurship, and focus on the timeless values necessary to succeed."

~ ***Entrepreneur Magazine***

Made in the USA
Middletown, DE
06 July 2018